THE ARMENIANS IN AMERICA

ETHNIC CHRONOLOGY SERIES
NUMBER 27

The Armenians in America
1618-1976
A Chronology & Fact Book

Compiled and edited by

Vladimir Wertsman

1978
OCEANA PUBLICATIONS, INC.
DOBBS FERRY, NEW YORK

Library of Congress Cataloging in Publication Data

Wertsman, Vladimir, 1929-
   The Armenians in America, 1618-1976.

   (Ethnic chronology series)
   Bibliography: p.
   Includes index.
   SUMMARY: A chronology of the Armenians in America
accompanied by pertinent documents.
      1. Armenian Americans—History—Chronology.
2. Armenian Americans—History—Sources. [1. Armenian
Americans—History] I. Title II. Series.
E184.A7W47   973'.04'91992   77-20704
ISBN 0-379-00529-8

Manufactured in the United States of America

TABLE OF CONTENTS

More than three and a half centuries have elapsed since
the first Armenian set foot on American soil. Today, the Armenian Americans comprise an ethnic community of about 500,000 people spread all over the United States, but mainly concentrated in
the states of California, Illinois, Massachusetts, Michigan, New
Jersey, New York, Ohio, Pennsylvania, and Rhode Island. Armenian
Americans have a strong and proud feeling of their national identity and historical heritage, undefatigable struggle against oppression, and love for freedom. They inherited these traits from
their ancestors who — during their multi-thousand year history
— were often victims of foreign invasions and subjected to religious, political or national persecutions, repressions or mass
extermination. The majority of Armenian Americans belong to the
Armenian Church, an independent branch of the Eastern Orthodox
Church, founded by St. Gregory the Illuminator in the year 301
A.D. The remaining Armenians are Catholics and Protestants. The
Armenian language is the only surviving branch of the Indo-European group of languages, and is written in a special Armenian
alphabet created by St. Mesrop and St. Sahak around the year 400
A.D. Armenian Americans are intelligent, hard workers, corageous,
enterprising, witty, flexible, and have made substantial contributions to our country, especially in the fields of industry,
business, medicine, education, literature, science, music, arts,
and entertainment. Alex Manoogian (industry), Gullabi Gulbenkian
(business), Dr. Varastad Kazandjian (medicine), James Tashjian
(education), Harry Daghlian (science), William Saroyan (literature), Alan Hovhaness (music), John Garo (photography), Rouben
Mamoulian (movies), Housep Pushman (painting), Rouben Nakian
(sculpture), Arman Tokatyan (opera), Mike Connors (television)
are only a few from a list of numerous prominent Armenian American personalities who are going to be met in this book.
    The present volume was designed to serve as a textbook
providing basic information on Armenian Americans. It contains
a chronology of significant events in the life of Armenian Americans, important documents related to the events, an annotated
bibliography broadening the sphere for further research, and an
appendix consisting of a list of Armenian American institutions
and organizations, influential periodicals, Armenian proverbs and
sayings, as well as short biographies of Armenian American personalities, recipients of the Bicentennial Award of Excellence
for their services to America and the Armenian American community. Although intended primarily as an introduction to reference materials for secondary school and community college students, the book can also be used as a valuable aid to teachers,
researchers, and other categories of readers interested in ethnic
studies.
    In preparing this book, I have received the assistance

of the Armenian Apostolic Church of America, Armenian General
Benevolent Union of America, Armenian Literary Society, Armenian
Library and Museum of America, Armenian Missionary Association of
America, Armenian Relief Society, Brooklyn Public Library, Colum-
bia University Libraries, Immigration History Research Center Un-
iversity of Minnesota, New York Public Library, and the University
of California, Los Angeles Library. I am especially indebted to
Dr. Fred Assadourian, Dr. G. H. Chapourian, Ms. M. Cheteyan, Mr.
K. N. Magarian and Professor Richard Hovannisian for their out-
standing help. I am also grateful to Mr. Lester Annenberg, Mrs.
Orit Barna, Mrs. Arpie Demerjian, Mrs. Shirley Goldberg, Mr.
Lemuel Kiretchjian, Mr. Asfadour Mardirosian, Dr. Aleksander
Sokolyshin and Mr. Paul Zaplitny for their fruitful cooperation
during various stages of my research.

Vladimir Wertsman
Brooklyn Public Library
Brooklyn, New York

CHRONOLOGY

1618-19   The first Armenian presence on American soil was
           recorded. Martin the Armenian, also known and re-
           corded in documents as "Martin the Armeanean" or
           "Martin Ye Armenia" came to Jamestown, Virginia,
           together with other settlers — members of the
           Virginia Company of London. It was assumed that
           Martin was one of Governor George Yeardley's ser-
           vants.

1623   Martin the Armenian, originally stemming from Persia,
           acquired British citizenship, and became a member of
           the standing committee of the Virginia Company of
           London.

1653   Edward Diggs, a noted leader of the Colony of Vir-
           ginia, brought two Armenians from Turkey, at his
           own expense. The two Armenian immigrants had "a
           high reputation in their native land for their skill
           and experience in the raising of silk worms."

1656   December. The Assembly of Virginia passed a resolu-
           tion permitting George the Armenian — one of the
           two immigrants who arrived in 1653 — to have 4,000
           pounds of tobacco in order to encourage him "in the
           trade of silk and to stay in the country."

1682   Stephen Zadori (derived from Zadoorian, meaning,
           "Given by God" in Armenian), a noted scholar prob-
           ably from Hungary, visited the Colony of New Eng-
           land. The permission to visit America, where
           Zadori spent six months, was facilitated by the
           Archbishop of Canterbury, England.

1719   Reverend Peter Tustian was appointed and served as
           minister of the Parish of St. George in South Car-
           olina. He later moved to Maryland.

1738   December 9. Stephen Tarrian, also known as
           Stephen Tarrien, was one of the signers of a
           petition addressed to the trustees of the Colony
           of Georgia.

1834   The first Armenian mass immigration to America be-
           gan. Khachadour Osnagyan, a student of the Ameri-
           can Missionary School in Istanbul (Constantinople),
           Turkey, came to the United States, and settled in
           New York City. He graduated from the City College
           of New York, became journalist, and later was
           elected president of the New York Press Club.
           Osnagyan started a pro American immigration move-
           ment among Armenian students in Turkey, and as a
           result several Armenian students came to the United

States to further their education in the following decades.

1843   Christopher Der Seropian, an Armenian student from Turkey, came to the United States and went to Yale University, where he introduced the class book custom. He was also credited with the development of the black and green colors used to this day on United States paper money.

1845-50   Individual Armenian immigrants from Turkey, mostly students, continued to come to the United States for academic purposes, but after the completion of studies, many returned to their native country. Among them was Rev. Haroutune Vahabedian, who studied at the Union Theological Seminary in New York City, and later became a Patriarch.

1851   Khachadour Osganyan published a book entitled, The Sultan and His Peoples directed against Turkish oppression of different ethnic groups, among which Armenians occupied a leading place. It was the first English written book by an Armenian American printed in the United States.

1861-64   Thomas Corwin, of Armenian-Hungarian parentage, distinguished himself in the State of Ohio, as an orator, lawyer, secretary of treasury, and governor. He also was elected as U.S. Congressman, and later served as U.S. Minister to Mexico.

During the Civil War, about thirty Armenians fought on the side of the Union. There were also three doctors — Simon Minasian, Bornig Mataosian, and I. Calousdian — who served in Philadelphia hospitals.

1851-70   Statistical records show that about fifty new Armenian immigrants arrived in the United States. Some of them were students, but the majority came to learn trades. This new trend was attributed to Dr. Cyrus Hamlin, founder of the Robert College in Istanbul, Turkey, who advocated the idea of teaching Turkish natives modern methods of industry.

1867   Garo, a servant of missionary George C. Knapp, was the first Armenian settler in Worcester, Massachusetts. In the following years, Massachusetts became the home to thousands of Armenian American immigrants.

1870-75   Dozens of new Armenian immigrants arrived in the

United States from Turkey, and most of them settled
in New York City. Others were scattered in Jersey
City, New Jersey, and in Rochester, New York. It
was the result of expanded American missionary work
in the Armenian provinces and letters sent by previous immigrants.

1876-77   The Armenian headquarters in Istanbul (Constantinople), Turkey was burned and looted by Turkish
soldiers and policemen. It marked the beginning of
persecutions against the Armenians in Turkey, and
an expression of the wrath of Sultan Abdul-Hamid II,
who had just came to power and strongly opposed the
Armenian nationalist movement. In order to escape
persecutions, many refugees, especially students
belonging to the Hunchakian Party (Social Democrats)
left Turkey for the United States. They continued
their studies at Yale, Princeton, Amherst, New York,
and other universities.

1884   Dr. John Topkahanian and Haigaz Eginian together
with other immigrants founded the New Jersey Armenian community.

1888   May. Arekag (Sun), the first Armenian newspaper in
the United States, was published in Jersey City, New
Jersey, by Haigaz Eginian. It had a very limited
circulation, and it changed its name to Soorhantag
(Messenger). Later the name was again changed to
Azadootun (Freedom).

1889   As the persecutions and physical maltreatment of
Armenians continued in Turkey, the number of Armenian immigrants to the United States kept increasing. In the next few years, the Armenian community considerably expanded, and was estimated to
be about 3,000.

The newly arrived immigrants founded small settlements
in or around New York City, Worcester, Lynn and Boston, Massachusetts, Hartford, Connecticut, Philadelphia, Pennsylvania, Chicago, Illinois, and Fresno,
California.

An Armenian bishop from Istanbul (Constantinople),
Turkey, was dispatched to the United States to organize the Armenian parishes in America. They fell
under the jurisdiction of the Holy Etchmiadzin See.
Etchmiadzin is the historical cathedral built by
Gregory the Illuminator in 301 A.D., in the vicinity
of Yerevan, capital of Armenia, presently part of
the Soviet Union.

Due to specific historical conditions, the Armenian Church had also established another See in Cilicia, Turkey, and two Patriarchates, one in Constantinople, Turkey, and one in Jerusalem, Palestine, presently Israel.

1891 The Church of the Holy Saviour, the first Armenian Apostolic church in America, was built in Worcester, Massachusetts. It was headed by Fr. Housep Saratian.

1892 The first Armenian Protestant church in America, named Martyr's Church, was also built in Worcester, Massachusetts.

1894-96 The second wave of Armenian mass immigration to America began. A series of barbaric massacres in Turkey took the lifes of about 250,000 Armenians, and earned Sultan Abdul-Hamid II the infamous ephitet of "The Red Sultan." A new wave of Armenians left Turkey for the United States, and joined their conationals in already established Armenian American settlements.

1895 A newspaper called Gaidsak (Lightening) started publication in Lynn, Massachusetts, but had an existence of a few months only.

1896 Fresno, California, received its first Armenian immigrants, and the Armenian Evangelical Church was founded in New York City.

1897 Digris (Tigris), a newspaper founded by H. Eginian and T. Charshafjian, soon changed its name to Tzaln Hayarenyatz (Voice of the Fatherland) and became the official organ of the Hunchakian Party.

1898 The semi-weekly newspaper Yeprad (Euphrates), was published in Worcester, Massachusetts, but soon ceased publication.

1899 Hairenik (Fatherland), the oldest Armenian daily in the United States, was published by the Dashnagtzagan Party, which later changed its name to the Armenian Revolutionary Federation of America. The newspaper is the organ of this party and covers national, international, local and group news affecting Armenian Americans.

Madiros Mighirian, the first Armenian Catholic priest in the United States, arrived in America and ministered in Boston. Armenian Catholic parishes were

later formed in Paterson, New Jersey, Philadelphia,
Pennsylvania, and Watertown, Massachusetts.

1900   Immigration authorities recorded 70,982 Armenian immigrants to the United States during the last five
years. They mainly settled in Massachusetts, New
York, Rhode Island, and California.

1901   Looys (Light), a very good journal devoted to
scientific, philosophic, and cultural aspects of
life, was published by M. Minassian, but did not
last more than five years.

1902   September 2. The existent parishes of the Armenian
Church in the United States were organized into a
diocese under the jurisdiction of the Holy Etchmiadzin. (see 1889)

1903   The Hunchakian Party in America put out Yeristasard
Hayastan (Young Armenia) as its official organ. The
publication, which is still in existence, appears as
a weekly and covers general and political news. The
Hunchakians are social democrats.

1905   Haig Patigian, noted sculptor of San Francisco,
California, created the McKinley monument in Arcata,
California. Patigian's important pieces of art in-
clude, among others, the figures of "Invention,"
"Imagination," "Steam Power," and "Electricity Power"
at the Rowell monument in Fresno, California.
Patigian was accepted as member of the National
Sculpture Society, and of the American Federation of
Arts.

1906   The Armenian General Benevolent Union of America
(AGBU) came into existence as a branch of an international charitable organization founded by Bogos
Nubar, world famous Armenian politician and philantropist of Egypt. Its innitial aim was to help
Armenian refugees all over the world. The Union is
presently the largest and most representative organization of the Armenian Americans, and it is involved in charitable, cultural, and educational activities. It is committed to preserving the Armenian heritage and to maintain the national integrity
of the Armenians in their homeland, and acts as an
umbrella organization tending to unify all Armenians
regardless of sex, political beliefs or place of
residence.

1907   The Armenian Constitutional Democratic Party started
publishing Ask (Nation) while the Reorganized

Hunchakian Party (a group that broke away from the
Hunchakian Party) put out <u>Bahag</u> (Sentinel) as their
official organs.

1907   The Armenian Revolutionary Federation of California
published <u>Asbarez</u> (Arena Stage), a semi-weekly which
has presently a circulation of about 1,000 copies.
It is devoted to international, national, cultural
and scientific aspects of life. It also carries
political, educational, religious articles, and its
main aim is to disseminate Armenian culture, to shed
light on the state of Armenians worldwide, and to
help achieve the goal of an "independent free and
united Republic of Armenia."

1908   August 31. William Saroyan, one of America's distinguished and popular authors and playrights, was
born in Fresno, California.

1909   The massacre of Armenians in Turkey was resumed with
renewed fury by the Young Turks, this time in the
province of Cilicia. 30,000 Armenians were killed,
and the massacre was arrested only after the intervention of the Great Powers, including the United
States. A new wave of Armenian refugees came to the
United States and settled in or around Armenian
American centers.

Paolo Ananian, a basso singer, joined the Metropolitan Opera House in New York City, and distinguished
himself in many roles during the next decade. He
also performed for the Boston Company.

1910   The Armenian Red Cross Society was founded with the
purpose of collecting and distributing money for relief of Armenians around the world, and for advancement of cultural activities. The society, consisting of women only from different countries, helped
thousands of Armenian Americans in resolving the re-
settling problems. It also accorded food, clothing
and educational assistance.

The Armenian Students Association was established to
provide scholarships and loans to students of Armenian descent. It is still in existence, with about
1,000 members, and besides scholarships and fellow-
ships given to deserving students, it also presents
awards (Kabakjian Award and Sarafian Award) in the
fields of citizenship and science to notable Armenian Americans. It puts out a quarterly newsletter,
a yearly directory as well as a yearly convention
pamphlet.

1911   Flora Zabelle (born Mangasarian), of Chicago, Illin-
            ois, a noted musical and screen star, co-stared with
            Raymond Hitchcok, her husband and producer, in The
            Red Widow, presented in the Astor Theater in New
            York City. She later appeared in movies and became
            a life member of Actors Fund.

1912   The Armenian Evangelical Church of New York started
            publishing Amsatertik (Monthly Bulletin), a bi-
            lingual monthly publication covering religious and
            general news of interest to parishioners. Presently
            it has a circulation of 1,200 copies.

1914-16   Because of the Armenian symphathies for the Allied
            cause during World War I, the Turkish authorities
            organized mass deportations of Armenians to the
            Syrian desert, accompanied by unprecedented mass-
            acres. This genocide action physically destroyed
            about 1,800,000 Armenians, forced thousands to con-
            vert to Islamism, and caused about 1,000,000 Ar-
            menians to flee in panic to other countries.

            The policy of the Turkish Government to exterminate
            Armenians was strongly protested by Henry Morgenthau,
            the United States Ambassador in Turkey, at that time.
            It aroused the indignation among the American people,
            and lead to the formation of the Near East Relief,
            chaired by Henry Morgenthau. America became more
            aware of the Armenian plight, and acted accordingly
            by granting assylum to thousands of Armenian ill-
            fated refugees.

1915   The Armenian General Benevolent Union of America
            started publishing Hoosharar (The Trompeter), a
            fraternal publication, which initially appeared
            in the Armenian language only. Presently it is
            published in Armenian and English, and it has a
            circulation of about 10,000 copies monthly.

            Philip Bennyan, a very fine bariton, made his oper-
            atic debut with the National Grand Opera Company of
            Los Angeles, California. He soon became a leading
            American singer, appearing in more than twenty
            roles in the United States and abroad.

1917-1918   During World War I, after the United States joined
            the Allied forces, thousands of Armenian Americans
            volunteered in the U.S. Armed Forces. They were most
            numerous in the famed YD (Yankee Division) from
            Massachusetts. Lieutenant-Colonel H. Malejian and
            Major Varaztad Kazanjian distinguished themselves in
            the U.S. Army Medical Services.

1918   September. Private First Class Vartan Aghababian of the 146th Infantry Regiment, U.S. Infantry Division, displayed exceptional bravery and heroism during the American offensive in France. He was awarded the Distinguished Service Cross and the Congressional Medal of Honor, and became the first Armenian American to receive such high honors. During his military service, Aghababian was wounded fourteen times.

The Armenian Evangelical Association of America came into existence as an organization of ministers and laymen of Armenian churches in the United States and abroad interested in missions. During the following decades, its membership grew to 4,000 and became involved in child education sponsorships, management of the Haigizian College in Beirut, Lebanon, and publication activities. The name of the organization was later changed to the Armenian Missionary Association.

May 28. After defeating an invading Turkish army, the surviving Armenians residing in Eastern Anatolia and Cillcia, Turkey, set up and proclaimed an independent state called Republic of Armenia. The newly created state was strongly supported by Armenian Americans, by Armenians from other countries, and by the Allied Powers.

Mrs. Zarouhi Kalemkarian, a noted Armenian writer, known as "the Grand Old Lady of Armenian Belle Letters," came to the United States and continued her prolific literary activities. She contributed to several Armenian magazines with her poetry and novels.

1920   President Woodrow Wilson supported the independent Armenian state, and drew the definitive frontiers for Armenia with access to the Black Sea at Trebizond.

The Treaty of Sevres (France), signed by Turkey and the Allies, enlarged the territory of independent Armenia, and incorporated most of the historical Armenias. But in the same year, Russia and Turkey invaded Armenia and dismantled the independent state. Russia took over Eastern Armenia and proclaimed it as a Soviet Republic with Yerevan as its capital, while Turkey annexed Kars and Ardahan cities and provinces.

The disappearance of the Armenian independent state in tragic circumstances, caused tens of thousands of Armenians to leave their native places and look for asylum abroad. The new wave of Armenian dispersion brought about 30,000 Armenian immigrants to the United States between 1920 and 1930. They settled in Massachusetts, New York, Detroit, Michigan, Chicago, Illinois, and California.

Gullabi Gulbenkian, a noted businessman and philantropist, founded the Gullbenkian Foundation in New York City, for charitable and educational purposes. The foundation, which is still in existence, is involved in general giving, primarily in the Middle East, with emphasis on higher education, as well as in church and hospital supports. Presently it has assets of about $1,000,000.

Alex Manoogian, a prominent industrialist, philantropist and leader of the Armenian American community emmigrated from Turkey to the United States. Although only nineteen, he displayed an usual business acumen, and in a few years opened a factory in Detroit, Michigan, which later developed into the Masco Corporation.

1921   The St. James Armenian Church was established in Watertown, Massachusetts. During the following decades it grew from a small church into a large complex and important religious center.

The Armenian Women's Welfare Association was founded by a group of women interested in helping with charitable work. It maintains a nursing home for the aged, and presently has about 500 members.

Nor Or (New Day) started appearing in Los Angeles, California. It is still in existence, and it appears semi-weekly covering news in the Armenian language only. It has a circulation of about 1500 copies.

Horsep Pushman, noted painter of New York City, received a medal for his works of art exhibited in the famous Salon of Paris, France. Pushman's paintings were later acquired by the Milwaukee, Wisconsin and Minneapolis, Minnesota, museums of art.

Miran Karagheusian and other members of this family established The Howard Karagheusian Commemorative Corporation in New York City. The main goal of this foundation, which is still in existence, is to promote child welfare, public health services, and relief programs for Armenian refugee communities in Greece, Lebanon, Syria, and other moslem countries.

The present assets of the foundation are about
$7,000,000.

1922   The Baikar Association of Boston, Massachusetts,
        started publishing Baikar (Struggle), a daily re-
        sulted from the merger of the former Ask (Nation)
        and Bahag (Sentinel). Presently, it is the offi-
        cial publication of the Armenian Democratic Liberal
        Party, and it covers international, national, and
        local news, as well as events of special interest
        to Armenians. It has a circulation of about 2,000
        copies per issue.

1923   February 14. Armand Tokatyan, an internationally
        renowned operatic tenor, made his debut at the New
        York Metropolitan House as Lucio in Vittadini's
        Anima Allegra. He remained a valued member of the
        company during the following two decades. He also
        sang in San Francisco, Los Angeles, Chicago, and in
        several European countries.

        Akim Tamiroff, noted movie actor, came to the United
        States. He soon distinguished himself in the world
        of cinematography in dozens of movies. He started
        in Okay America, then in Queen Christina, later in
        Don Quixote, and several others.

1927   With the influx of new Armenian immigrants in Cali-
        fornia, the Armenian churches of that state formed
        a separate (Western) diocese under the jurisdiction
        of the Holy Etchmiadzin. The other churches be-
        longed to the Eastern Diocese under the same juris-
        diction. (See 1902)

        Rouben Mamoulian of Beverly Hills, California, noted
        stage and screen director, produced the play Porgy.
        It was Mamoulian's first production in New York City
        and it ran for more than two years. A few years
        later, Mamoulian's first movie, Applause, was also
        very successful. Mamoulian directed many other
        movies during the 1930's and 1940's.

1930   Arshile Gorky (Born Vosdanig Manoog Adoian), noted
        modern painter, exhibited three of his paintings at
        the Museum of Modern Art in New York City. He pre-
        viously attended as student and taught at the Grand
        Central School of Art where he became famous for
        original style. He previously studied at the Rhode
        Island School of Design and The Union of Marash
        Armenians started publishing Germanik (Little
        Germany) a quarterly bilingual (English and Armenian)
        mainly of local interest. Presently it has a cir-

culation of 1,000 copies.

1933   William Saroyan made his debut as writer with a
short story called "The Broken Wheel," which appeared in Hairenik, organ of the Armenian Revolutionary Federation of America.

Hairenik started publishing a weekly suplement in
English, in order to convey its political position
to the younger generation of Armenian Americans.
(see 1899)

A separation of jurisdictional powers occurred
within the Armenian Church in America. It was
generated by a dispute over the condition of the
Armenian Church in the Soviet Union. As a result
of the dispute, one group of Armenian American
parishes opted to remain under the jurisdiction of
the Holy See of Etchmiadzin, Armenia, while a second
group remained independent until it was later accepted under the jurisdiction of the Holy See of
Cilicia in Antelia, Lebanon. The separation of
jurisdictions did not affect the dogma and liturgy
of the Armenian Church.

The Hairenik Association of Boston, Massachusetts,
started publishing The Armenian Weekly to encourage
the concept of an independent Armenian state, and
to urge the retention of Armenian identity abroad.
The publication carries materials on social, cultural, political, and historical events, national
and international news, articles devoted to Armenian youth, and translations from the Armenian language press. It has a circulation of about 2,500
copies.

After the New Deal legislation was adopted, Reuben
Nakian, distinguished sculptor of Stamford, Connecticut, won his fame for his portrait busts devoted
to President Franklin Delano Roosevelt, Secretary
of State Cordell Hull, and other prominent political leaders of the time. He also produced later
an eight foot tall sculpture of Babe Ruth, noted
baseball player.

1934   William Saroyan published his first book consisting
of twenty-six short stories entitled The Daring
Young Man of the Flying Trapeze and Other Stories.
The book soon became a best seller.

The Baikar Association of Watertown, Massachusetts,
published The Armenian Mirror-Spectator, a weekly

concerned with keeping alive "the consciousness of
the Armenian Cultural heritage." It covers cultural
and religious aspects of the Armenian community, and
it presently has a circulation of 2,700.

1935   The Educational Association of Malatia, located in
            Cleveland, Ohio, published a quarterly called Pap
            Oukhti (Grand Father's Devotion), which is still in
            existence and has a circulation of 500.

1937   Leon Danielian, noted dancer and choreographer, made
            his debut in the United States with the Mordkin
            Ballet. Later he danced in I Married An Angel, a
            musical by Rogers and Hart, and performed in several
            other shows.

            The Armenian Progressive League of America, a left-
            ist organization, issued Lraper (The Armenian
            Herald), a semi-weekly covering international,
            national, and local news. It is a bilingual publi-
            cation (Armenian and English) and presently has a
            circulation of about 2,400.

            Arlene Frances, born Kazanjian, noted stage and
            movie actress, and television personality, started
            her career in the play called Two Women. She later
            successfully appeared in Horse Eats Hat and Danton's
            Death, two Orson Wells Mercury Theater productions.

1938   Tamara Toumanova, one of the original ballerinas of
            Swan Lake, appeared for the first time in New York
            City, dancing in Stars in Your Eyes, a Broadway
            musical. Later she appeared in some movies as Anna
            Pavlova, world renowned Russian Ballerina. She also
            made guest appearances with several American compan-
            ies, including the American Ballet Theater.

            The Diocese of the Armenian Church of America star-
            ted the publication of Hayastanyaitz Yegeghetzy (The
            Armenian Church), a monthly which was issued only in
            Armenian during the following two decades. It pri-
            marily covers religious news, but also includes
            articles on Armenian literature and history.
            Presently it has a circulation of over 6,000 copies.

            The Red Cross Society published Hai Sird (Armenian
            Heart), a bilingual (Armenian and English) quarterly
            intended as an informative propaganda, and mainly
            addressed to its members, sympathizers, and contrib-
            utors. It contains articles related to the history
            of the organization, purposes, and meetings. Occa-
            sionally, it publishes fiction or poetry in either

language, and presently its circulation is about
1,500.

St. Gregory the Illuminator Church of New York City,
an important religious and cultural center of the
Diocese of the Armenian Church of America published
Lousarovich (The Illuminator), a bilingual weekly
covering church and parish affairs news. Its
present circulation is about 1,000.

Emmanuel Varandyan published The Well of Ararat, an
exotic novel of Persian Armenian life. It won the
Avery Hopwood Contest Award.

Artin Shalian published Pagan Idylls, an original
literary work reflecting the allegorical basis of
the Armenian culture.

1939   Alan Hovhanness (born Chakmakjian) of Sommerville,
            Massachusetts, noted contemporary composer, became
            known for his Symphony No. 1 performed by the BBC
            Symphony under the conductor, Leslie Howard. A few
            years later, Hovhannes produced Armenian Rhapsody
            No. 2.

            William Saroyan's play The Time of Your Life opened
            on Broadway in New York City. It was so successful
            that its author won the Pulitzer Prize of the year.
            A year later Saroyan won acclaim for his book My
            Name Is Aram, an imaginary description of an Arme-
            nian boy's life in California.

1940   St. Illuminator's Armenian Apostolic Church of New
            York City published Mair Yegeghetzi (Mother Church),
            a monthly devoted to Armenian church affairs, spe-
            cial services, donations, weddings, baptisms, and
            funerals. It is still in existence, has a circu-
            lation of 1,200, and it is distributed free of
            charge.

            Rouben Mamoulian's movie Mark of Zorro was very suc-
            cessful with film audiences. It was followed by
            Rings On Her Fingers, and Summer Holidays.
            Mamoulian's talent consisted in blending movement,
            dancing, action, music, singing, decor, and light-
            ing into one setting entity.

1941-44   During World War II, 20,000 Armenian Americans, rep-
            resenting about ten percent of the Armenian American
            total population of that period, served with the
            United States Army, Navy, Coast Guard, Marine Corps,
            and paramilitary units. Hundreds of Armenian Ameri-

cans gave their lives in action, thousands were
wounded, and several thousands received decorations
for bravery. Corporal James M. Topazian was the
first Armenian American killed in action during
World War II. After the end of the war, a street
was named in his honor by the citizens of Boston,
Massachusetts. Lieutenant Ernest Devrishian of
Richmond, Virginia, received the Congressional
Medal of Honor for heroic action in Italy. Lieutenant I. Kousharian was the first American who
died in the invasion of Africa. Colonel Sarkis M.
Zartarian of Arlington, Massachusetts, and Lieutenant Ernest Dervishian of Richmond, Virginia were
awarded the Congressional Medal of Honor. Com-
manders Jack (Sirak) Nahigian and Edward Barsumian
of Chicago, Illinois, were awarded the Purple Heart
with Gold Star for bravery in the Pacific operations. Dsaghig and Manishag Aslanian, of Olean,
New York, were the first twin sisters to serve with
the Women's Army Corps. WAC Staff Sargeant Sue
Sarafian of Detroit, Michigan, served as secretary
of General Dwight Eisenhower.

1941   Yusuf Karsh, a noted photographer of New York City
and Canada, became famous for his portrait of Winston Churchill, prime minister of Great Britain.
He later worked for Life magazine, and his powerful
portraits of statesmen, scientists, and political
leaders from the United States and abroad, became
an integral part of contemporary history. Karsh
was trained by John H. Garo of Boston, Massachusetts, another Armenian American photographer of
distinction.

Anne Avakian-Bishop of Los Angeles, California, dis-
tinguished herself as a war correspondent for the
New York News-Chicago Tribune Syndicate. She later
interviewed international personalities such as
Charles DeGaulle, Winston Churchill, Pope John
XXIII, and many others.

1942   January. Haig Shekerjian was appointed brigadier
general by order of President Franklin Delano
Roosevelt. Shekerjian distinguished himself in the
Chemical Warfare Service and was the first Armenian
American to be elevated to the rank of general.

H. Ajemian (Ariel), noted painter of New York City,
executed the murals in the Roxbury, Massachusetts,
cathedral, and his art is considered one of the
finest in America.

Alex Manoogian, noted philantropist and businessman, founded the Alex and Marie Manoogian Foundation in Troy, Michigan. The foundation primarily supports welfare and religious institutions, higher and secondary education, with emphasis on music and arts. Its assets exceed $21,000,000, and it is considered to be the strongest Armenian American foundation by its financial position, and the impacts of accorded assistance. (see 1920)

1943   Alan Hovhaness became a faculty member of the Boston Conservatory of music, and taught until 1951. During this period he composed Anahid, Saint Vartan Symphony, and several pieces inspired by Armenian themes.

1945   August 23. Atomic scientist Harry K. Daghlian, of New London, Connecticut, lost his life while conducting an after hour experiment with U-235 and plutonium, explosives that went into the atomic bomb. The fatal incident occurred at the Los Alamos, New Mexico, laboratory.

Leon (Zaven) Surmelian, of Los Angeles, California, published I Ask You, Ladies and Gentlemen, a very successful auto-biographical work, telling the gruesome, tragic, and triumphant story of the Armenian massacres. In the same year, he became a junior screen writer for Metro-Goldwyn-Meyer studios.

At the end of World War II, groups of Armenian immigrants, especially from France, Egypt, Irak, Iran, and Lebanon, started a new wave of immigration to the United States.

1946   The Armenian Red Cross Society changed its name to the Armenian Relief Society (ARS). The American branch of the society has its main headquarters in Boston, Massachusetts, and reunites more than 3,000 members in the United States and Canada. Besides its assistance to needy Armenian refugees, it awards scholarships to needy students, sends students abroad to study at Armenian education centers, and also operates thirty-six Armenian classes in the United States. In addition, it sponsors clinics, orphanages, concerts, lectures, and other cultural activities.

The Armenian Church Youth Organization of America (ACYOA) was founded by the Armenian Church of America. It presently has a membership of about 1,500 young men and women between the ages of fourteen and twenty-six, and conducts religious, educational, cultural, social, and recreational programs. It also accords scholarships to deserving students and puts out The Armenian Guardian, a monthly concerned with religious materials as well as with news regarding the events sponsored by the organization.

Brigadier General Haig Shekerjian, the first Armenian American general in the history of the United States, retired from active duty, after devoting thirty-nine years to army service. The last year of his active duty, he spent as commanding general of Camp Silbert, Alabama.

1947

The Hairenik Association of Boston, Massachusetts, started the publication of The Armenian Review, a quarterly literary-historical devoted to Armenian culture and civilization. It contains historical articles, memoirs, political studies, short stories, poetry, book reviews, editorials, translations from significant Armenian materials, and its main objective is to support the Armenian quest for an independent, free, united, and democratic Armenian state. It has a circulation of about 1,000.

The Isadore and Sunny Familian Foundation was established in Beverly Hills, California, with primary emphasis on local giving, medical, religious, and community welfare. It presently has assets of about $1,250,000.

Samuel Toumanyan of New York City, started publishing a private weekly called Nor Ashkar Weekly (The New World Weekly), which is still in existence and appears in Armenian and English. It has a circulation of about 1,000.

1948

January 19. Hurach B. Abajian of Franklin, Massachusetts, had been awarded the Medal of Freedom for his work in a civil capacity with the United States Army in the Pacific during World War II.

The American National Committee to Aid Homeless Armenians was founded in San Francisco, California, with the purpose of helping and assisting Armenian refugees from Eastern European and other countries to resettle in the United States, Canada, South America, and Australia.

The Armenian Home for the Aged was opened by the Armenian Welfare Association in New York City. During the next decade, the home became known for its

high quality care accorded to elderly Armenian
Americans. There are Armenian nursing homes in
Boston, Los Angeles, and other places.

Arshile Gorky, noted painter, took his life at the
age of forty-three in New York City. In his last
years, he adopted and was famous for his surrealistic style. Gorky's paintings were purchased by the
Whitney Museum of American Art in New York City.

1950   The Armenian Educational Foundation was established
            in Los Angeles, California, with the purpose of
            rendering financial assistance to Armenian schools
            in the United States and countries friendly to the
            United States.

            Lucine Amara (born Armaganian), noted soprano singer,
            made her debut at the Metropolitan Opera in New York
            City. She had appeared as Celestial Voice in Don
            Carlos. A few years later, she had a sensational
            success as Nevada in I Pagliacci and in several
            other roles. She also appeared extensively abroad.

1950-52   During the Korean War, many Armenian Americans dis-
            tinguished themselves on the battle field, and some
            gave their life for the cause of freedom. Private
            First Class Karnig Poryazian of West New York, New
            Jersey was the first Armenian American to die in the
            Korean War. Jet fighter Stephen (Stepy) Stepanian
            of Providence, Rhode Island, received the Distin-
            guished Service Cross and the Air Medal with two
            Oak Leaf Clusters. Major Roger H. Terzian of
            Fresno, California, was awarded the Bronze Star
            Medal.   John Najarian, of Fresno, California,
            one of the Nation's outstanding fliers, was also
            highly decorated.

1951   September 11. George Mardikian, a noted restauran-
            teur of San Francisco, California, received the
            Medal of Freedom, the highest civilian award of the
            Nation, for his special contribution in providing
            better food service for American combat troops in
            Korea.

            Hagop Kevorkian of New York City established the
            Hagop and Marjorie Kevorkian Foundation to promote
            interest in Near and Middle Eastern Art through ex-
            hibitions, scholarships, and fellowships for re-
            search and study in the field. The foundation's
            assets are around $6,750,000.

1952   Richard Hagopian, a gifted New England writer, pub-

lished Faraway the Spring, a very good novel devoted
to the life of Armenian American immigrants struggling to make their place in society. Hogopian
later published another book entitled Wine for the
Living.

After receiving her doctoral degree from Cornell
University, Pergrouhi Svajian became United Nations
consultant on women's education. Later she was
named research coordinator for the Ford Foundation,
and actively participated in the Armenian American
community life.

Mike Connors (born Krekor Ohanian) of Fresno, California, noted movie actor and television personality, made his debut in the film Sudden Fear. He
later appeared in several other movies, and became
very popular in Mannix, a television series for
which he received the Golden Globe Award.

Yeram Sarkis Touloukian, a scientist of West
Lafayette, Indiana, was appointed director of information and numerical data analysis and synthesis.
He later taught at different universities and was
promoted to high U.S. Government positions.

1953   Alex Manoogian, well known industrialist and philantropist, became the president of the Armenian
General Benevolent Union, the largest Armenian
American organization. Besides his generosity,
humanity, and humility, Alex Manoogian displayed an
excellent knowledge of the Armenian language, and
special interest in the preservation of Armenian
cultural heritage.

Rouben Mamoulian was elected vice president of the
Dramatologists Guild of America. During the past
two decades he won several national and international film prizes, honorary citations, and other honors
for such films as Dr. Jekyll and Mr. Hyde, Carousel,
Blood and Sand.

1954   The National Association for Armenian Studies and
Research (NAASR) was founded in Cambridge, Massachusetts, to foster the study of Armenian history,
culture and language on an active, scholarly, and
continuous basis in America. It has established
chairs of Armenian studies at Harvard University
and University of California, Los Angeles University, as well as a full time program at Columbia
University, New York City. The Association maintains a library of about 500 volumes on various

aspects of Armenian history, culture, language, music, art, church history, and archaeology. It has about 2,500 members, and puts out a quarterly report and a Bulletin for the Advancement of Armenian Studies.

1955   Aram Tolegian of Los Angeles, California, was appointed chairman of the Human Relations Council of the Los Angeles Board of Education. He distinguished himself as teacher and university lecturer and published a book on Armenian folk epic.

Dick Minasian became director and professor of Engineering Logistics at the Naval School-Civil Engineer Corp Officers at Port Hueneme, California. He has a long and outstanding record of teaching American engineering military cadre.

The St. Grigor Lousarovitch Armenian Apostolic Church in Pasadena, California, started publishing Shoghakat (Radiance), a quarterly concerned with religious affairs.

Fred Ayvasian, a physician of Leonia, New Jersey, published Much Ado About Murder, a collection of detective stories a la Conan Doyle. He often used the pen name of Fred Levon.

1956   The Armenian Literary Society was founded in Yonkers, New York, with the purpose of helping Armenian authors morally and financially by promoting and distributing their publications, organizing lectures about Armenian literature and culture, and other activities. The society has about 400 members, collects and sends books to needy libraries, schools and student organizations in the United States and abroad. It also compiles bibliographic lists on Armenia and Armenians, and puts out Kir-Ou-Kirk (Letter and Book), a semi-annual publication in Armenian and English, covering the world of Armenian literature, as well as news regarding meetings, programs, and other activities led by the society. The circulation of this publication is about 2,500, and it is free of charge.

Garabed and Frances Paelian, a father and daughter literary team, published Anahid, a novel devoted to ancient Armenia.

1957   The group of Armenian parishes, which in 1933 refused the jurisdiction of the See of the Holy Etchmiadzin, was accepted under the jurisdiction

of the See of Cilicia, presently located in Antelia,
a suburb of Beirut, Lebanon. It adopted the name of
The Armenian Apostolic Church of America. The group
of parishes which remained under the jurisdiction of
the See of Etchmiadzin took the name of the Diocese
of the Armenian Church of America.

Leon Danielian joined the San Francisco, California,
Ballet. He was already a well established dancer
and coreographer, appreciated for his appearances
in Swan Lake, Les Sylphides, Carnaval, and other
ballets.
Peter Sourian, a graduate of Harvard University,
published Miri, and Marjorie Housepian, a graduate
of Barnard College, New York, published A Houseful
of Love, a very successful novel devoted to typical
Armenian life in America.

1958   The Diocese of the Armenian Church of America started
publishing Armenian Church, a monthly publication
with a circulation of about 6,000, devoted to church
affairs, organization, meetings, and other activities. It is an extension of Hayastanyaitz
Yegeghetzy.

St. Peter Armenian Apostolic Church of Van Nuys,
California, published Bari Lour (Good News), and
St. Sahak and St. Mesrop Armenian Apostolic Church
of Providence, Rhode Island, published Paros (Light-
house). Both publications are bilingual (Armenian
and English), they appear monthly, free of charge,
and mainly carry news of interest to the respective
parishioners.

Gabriel (Antoine) Vahanian, a noted scholar in
theology, joined the Department of Religion at
Syracuse University, New York. He is known for
his research and writings and was awarded a fellowship by the American Council of Learned Societies.

1959   George Mason of Fresno, California, published The
California Courier, a weekly with a circulation of
about 3,000 mainly covering news and events of
special interest to Armenian Americans residing
in California.

Koren Der Harootian, a noted sculptor of Mount
Vernon, New York, completed a thirteen foot figure
of Christ and four Armenian Christian martyrs for
the facade of the Armenian Diocese and Cultural
Center of New York City. Previously he distinguished himself with a marble eagle at the United States

Pavilion at the Brussels, Belgium, World Fair, and
took part in several exhibits organized in America
and abroad.

1960   The Knar Armenian Choral Group was founded in Philadelphia, Pennsylvania. It honors prominent Armenian composers of the past and present, and is involved in concerts, as well as other cultural activities.

The Armenian Evangelical Church was founded by a
group of Armenian Evangelical families from the
Middle East. It is associated with the Evangelical Union of North America, and its doctrine puts
main emphasis on the bible.

Samuel Mardian, Jr., a construction company leader,
was elected mayor of Phoenix, Arizona. He was very
active in the Republican Party, and also was involved in the work of several cultural, philantropi-
cal, and civic organizations.

1961   Arlene Francis appeared in the movie One Two Three.
Later she distinguished herself in the plays Lion
In Winter, Pal Joey, Who Killed Santa Claus, and
became nationally known and appreciated for her
television shows "What's My Line," "Arlene Francis
Show," and radio programs "What's My Name," "Blind
Date, Emphasis." She also published a book called
That Certain Something.

Crosby Englizian, a Baptist clergyman of Portland,
Oregon, received the George Washington Honor Medal,
awarded by the Freedom's Foundation in the sermon
category. He contributed to several religious
periodicals and published a book about Park Street
Church of Boston.

George Nakhnikian, author of numerous books and
lecturer in philosophy, became chairman of the
Philosophy Department at Wayne State University.

1962   The Armenian Evangelical Association of North America started publishing Armenian-American Outlook, a
quarterly concerned with religious matters. The
publication had a circulation of about 5,000.

Anahid Ajemian (violonist) and Maro Ajemian (pianist)
two sisters and accomplished artists of New York
City, made a nation wide tour as a duo. Both
artists, who started their careers in the 1940's,
worked at the Julliard School, New York, as in-

structors and received several awards. During the
following years, they became reputed performers of
contemporary music by Alan Hovhaness, Pierre Boulez,
John Cage, and others.

St. Sargis Armenian Apostolic Church of New York
City published Shoghakat (Radiance), a bilingual
English and Armenian) bi-monthly devoted to parish
news.

1963   The Armenian Apostolic Church of America started
issuing Kilikia (Cilicia), a quarterly publication
written in Armenian and English covered mainly
religious subjects. Its circulation was about
4,500.

David Aloian, of Concord, Massachusetts, a teacher
and author of educational books, became headmaster
of the Concord Academy.

1964   Ara Berberian of South Field, Michigan, joined the
New York City Opera as principal basso. Well known
in the United States and abroad, he became a leading opera singer in the following years. Berberian
is holder of a law and economics degree, but never
went to music school.

Cher (born Cherylin Sarkisian) of El Centro, California, noted pop singer and television personality,
became very successful together with her husband
Sonny Bono in their own show called Sonny and Cher.
Cher and her husband showed a great sense of responsibility towards their fans, and openly advocated
against drugs. They made an anti-drug movie for
the government, and later became involved in
charity work and the fight against cerebral palsy.

Aram Saroyan, son of the noted writer William
Saroyan, started publishing Lines, a magazine of
poems. He later published individual volumes of
his own poems and contributed to different literary
publications.

Leon Surmelian was appointed professor of English
at the California State College, Los Angeles. He
published several writings devoted to Armenian folk
tales and contributed to Hairenik.

Aram Vartanian, author of several studies on Diderot
and Descartes, joined the New York University as
professor of French. He has been awarded fellow-
ships by the Ford Foundation, Guggenheim Foundation,

as well as a Fullbright Research Grant to study in
France.

Dr. Louise Nalbandian of Fresno, California, became
faculty member of the California State University.
She organized an Armenian program at the University
of California, Los Angeles, and published several
books on the Armenian revolutionary movement in
Turkey.

1965 Richard Zakharian was appointed professor of foreign
languages at the California State University, Northridge, California. His appointment was preceded by
several years of teaching in various colleges and
universities.

William S. Sahakian, professor and author of Dedham,
Massachusetts, published a book entitled Realms of
Philosophy. It was soon followed by another book
dealing with great philosophers.

1966 Nonny Hogrogian of New York City, noted children's
books writer and illustrator, received the Caldecott
Award for the book Always Room for One More. She
later received a second Caldecott Award for the
book One Fine Day. She is well known for her prolific and inspired graphic arts activities.

Dr. Richard Hovannisian of Los Angeles, California,
became chairman of the Armenian Monument Council.
He distinguished himself as an author on modern
Armenian history, and Armenian community and church
activist in California.

1967 The New York Philarmonic performed Symphony No. 19
by Alan Hovhannes, under Andre Kostelanetz. The
symphony was preceded by Meditation on Zeami performed at the beginning of the 1960's by the American Symphony under Leopold Stokowski.

Cathy Berberian, one of the foremost interpreters
of avantgarde music, sang for the Chicago Symphony
Orchestra. She is well known for her flexibility,
and she appeared in several American, as well as
foreign concerts.

Marjorie Housepian became associate dean of studies
at Barnard College, New York, after a very successful literary career. A few years later she published
the book called The Smirna Affair.

The Armenian Reporter, an English weekly, started

publication in New York City. It has a circulation
of about 3,500, and it sheds light on cultural,
social, and religious events concerning the Armenian
community in the United States and abroad. It also
publishes profiles of Armenian personalities, a cal-
endar of important coming events, views and opinions
expressed by readers, letters to the editor, as well
as obituaries.

1968   Alex Manoogian established a separate cultural fund
within the Armenian General Benevolent Union to aid
in the promotion of Armenian culture, education, and
language. It also helps writers and artists and
those engaged in other cultural endeavors, and makes
substantial donations to some American universities
for Armenian studies, translations of books from
Armenian into English, and acquisition of books.

St. Vartan Cathedral was officially inaugurated in
New York City by the Diocese of the Armenian Church
in America. It also serves as the official head-
quarter of the Diocese. Vartan was an Armenian
military chief who gave his life defending the
Christian faith and Armenian independence against
Persian invaders in the fifth century A.D. St.
Vartan's Day is an Armenian national holiday observed yearly on February 21.

Vahan Vartanian of Boston, Massachusetts, was elevated to the rank of U.S. Brigardier General.
Later he was promoted to the rank of U.S. Major
General, and appointed Adjutant General of the National Guard of Massachusetts. Vartanian has a
long and distinguished military career starting
with World War II.

Robert Miron Ajemian of New York City became assistant managing editor of Time-Life, Inc. He started
his journalistic career as a reporter for Life Magazine, and worked his way up during the last two
decades.

Theodore Karagheuzoff of Brooklyn, New York, was
named commissioner of traffic for New York City.
He made important innovations for traffic enforcement such as reversible bus lanes, the use of meter
maids, and others. When he was appointed traffic
head, he was only thirty-three years old, and considered the youngest career civil servant to become
commissioner.

Avedis Krikor Sanjian became professor of Armenian

at the University of California, Los Angeles. He
is known as a noted scholar on Armenian manuscripts,
and is a contributor to professional journals.

David Kherdian of Santa Fe, California, acquired the
Giligia Press. He started his career as a door-to-
door magazine salesman, but soon became field manager, then published poems, bibliographies, and rapidly advanced in the publishing business.

Richard Abcarian of San Fernando, California, was
appointed professor of English at Valley State
College, Northridge, California. He contributed to
various literary journals and wrote critical studies
on Richard Wright.

The Armenian Scientific Association of America
started publishing a <u>Bulletin</u> reflecting the activities of the Association. The publication appeared
semi-annually and had a circulation of 500.

1969   The Stephen Philibosian Foundation was established
            in Radnor, Pennsylvania, by the Armenian Missionary
            Association of America. It accords grants largely
            for child welfare, and supports higher and secondary
            Armenian education, as well as Armenian churches.
            Its assets are around $2,500,000.

            The Alex Manoogian School was opened in Southfield,
            Michigan. In the following years, it became a lead-
            ing institution in the development of Armenian stud-
            ies curricula for primary, junior and senior high
            school studies.

            A retrospective exhibit of Reuben Nakian's works was
            opened at the Museum of Modern Art in New York City.
            His works are included in the permanent collections
            of this museum of the New School Art Center, New
            York. Previously, Nakian exhibited in different
            art centers all over the United States.

1970s   A new wave of Armenian immigrants to the United
            States began. The immigrants came from the Soviet
            Union and Middle Eastern countries, especially from
            Lebanon, where the civil war between Moslems and
            Christians gravely affected the Armenian community
            of this country.

1970   Dr. Vaharn Norair Dadrian was appointed professor of
            philosophy at the State University of New York, at
            Geneseo, New York. He previously taught at several
            other universities and colleges, contributed to

professional journals, and received several awards
and grants.

1972   According to official statistics, the Diocese of the
              Armenian Church of America had under its jurisdic-
              tion fifty-eight Armenian American churches with a
              membership of about 375,000, while the Armenian
              Apostolic Church of America had twenty-nine churches
              and 125,000 members. The Armenian Catholic member-
              ship was estimated to be around 8,000 concentrated
              mainly in six churches under the jurisdiction of
              local bishops. The Armenian Evangelical membership
              encompassed about 5,000 members.

              A noted movie actor Akim Tamiroff died at the age of
              seventy-three. He appeared in several dozens of
              movies, and his latest one was Then Came Bronson,
              two years before his death.

              The Armenian Assembly was set up in Washington, D.C.
              to maintain Armenian visibility in the nation's
              capital. It also serves as a center of distribu-
              tion of information on Armenian affairs, anti-defa-
              mation work, and supports all Armenian American or-
              ganization, as well as the entire community of
              Armenian Americans. It maintains a union catalog
              listing all books about Armenians in major American
              libraries, and biographical archives. It also is-
              sues a quarterly newsletter. The direction of the
              assembly was assumed by Avedis Sanjian and Dennis
              Papazian, both are university professors.

1973   Armen Tashdinian was named director of planning and
              analysis at the National Foundation of Arts and
              Humanities in Washington, D.C. He started his
              career as an intern a decade ago, moved quickly to
              the Office of Education, and then consistently
              worked his way up.

              Koren Der Harootian, noted sculptor, completed his
              twenty foot bronze sculpture with four relief panels
              for the Armenian Bicentennial Commemorative Commis-
              sion in Fairmont, Pennsylvania. Harootian is repre-
              sented in the permanent collections of the Metropol-
              itan Museum of Art and Whitney Art Museum in New
              York City, as well as in the Worcester Art Museum
              in Massachusetts.

              John K. Najarian was named probate judge in Johnston,
              Rhode Island. He later was appointed judge of the
              Rhode Island Family Court.

1974   Mrs. Margo Terzian Lang exhibited her paintings at
the Corcoran Museum in Washington, D.C., one of the
finest and oldest museums of our country. Her water-
colors enhance U.S. embassies all over the world,
and some of her works were acquired for the permanent collections of the Smithsonian Institution in
Washington, D.C.

William Saroyan's latest play, <u>Armenians</u>, was presented in the Armenian General Benevolent Union's
auditorium in New York City. The play is devoted
to a cross-section of the Armenian immigrants to the
United States, their problems of losing the national
heritage, and their children's Americanization.

Mr. Armais Artunoff, nationally prominent engineer,
was inducted into the Oklahoma Hall of Fame, for his
most outstanding achievments in the fields of
electro-mechanics and hydraulic engineering, as well
as for his invention of the famous electro-motor
submergible multi-stage centrifugal oil and water
pumping units. He is credited with more than sixty
patents in industrial equipment.

The Armenian Literary Society honored the late
Zarouhi Kalemkarian with a literary program devoted
to her works.

Attorney Suren Saroyan of San Francisco received the
"Man of the Year Award" from the American National
Committee to Aid the Homeless Armenians. He is
credited with the repatriation of 18,500 Armenians.
He helped settle 512 families in Los Angeles, Cali-
fornia.

1975   The Armenian American community and Armenian American organizations showed deep concern for the fate
of Armenians in Lebanon, a country profoundly
divided and gravely affected by the civil war between the Moslems and the Christians. As a result
of this conflict, many Armenians living in Lebanon
lost their lives, were wounded or remained homeless.
The Armenian American organizations and church institutions started a relief campaign to aid the
Armenians in Lebanon, and to help resettle those
Armenians who were admitted as immigrants to the
United States. Many of the newly arrived immigrants
settled in California.

April 24. Armenian Americans all over the United
States observed the sixtieth anniversary of the
Turkish massacres against Armenians during World

War I. The observance was specially dramatized in
New York City, with a population of about 50,000
Armenians, representing about one-tenth of the entire
Armenian community in the United States.

April. St. Nerses Shnorhali Library was opened in
New York City at the Headquarters of the Armenian
Apostolic Church of America. The library has about
2,500 books and was built mainly from donations.

August 24. Haik Kavookjian of New York City, probably the oldest living Armenian American, celebrated
his 100th birthday at a gala party organized and
attended by prominent Armenian American community
leaders from the United States and other countries.
Kavookjian preserved a very clear mind, good sense
of humor and looked young and energetic.

The Armenian Observer, a weekly covering major events
in the life of Armenian Americans living in California, started publication in Hollywood, California.

Dr. Winston L. Sarafian was named head of the
Library and director of the Learning Resources Center at Oxnard College, in Califirnia. Dr. Sarafian's
father (Dr. Armen Sarafian) and grand-father (Dr.
Kevork Sarafian) were also college professors and
heads of departments.

The Armenian Sisters Academy of Radnar, Pennsylvania,
a Montessori school, completed the construction of a
new building, with the help of several charitable
donations made by Armenian American organizations
and philantropists.

The United Armenian Commemorative Film Committee of
Los Angeles, California, produced two films devoted
to the Armenian massacres by the Turks during World
War I. The movies, The Armenian Case, and The
Forgotten Genocide, are very good documentaries.
They were directed by Dr. Michael Hagopian, as-
sited by Salpi Ghazarian, both of North Hollywood,
California.

1976   February 26. This day was proclaimed St. Vartan's
Day in the City of New York. St. Vartan, whose
real name was Vartan Mamoolian, fought against
Persian invaders and gave his life for the Armenian
national and religious cause in 451 A.D.

April 25. The Statue of Meher, an ancient Armenian
legendary hero, was unveiled near the Philadelphia

Museum of Fine Arts. The errection of the statue,
part of several manifestations during the country's
Bicentennial, is a symbol of gratitude the Armenian
Americans expressed for the United States. The
statue is the work of Khoren Der Horootian, noted
Armenian sculptor.

Congressman George E. Danielson, Democrat of California, has been named deputy majority whip in the
House of Representatives. He served as assistant
majority whip in the previous 92nd, 93rd, and 94th
Congress, and often came out as a strong spokesman
for the Armenian American community and its achievements.

George Deukmejian, noted Armenian American politician and statesman in California, was relected
state senator.

Rep. George Keverkian, Democrat of Everet, Massachusetts, is expected to perform significant tasks at
the State House in 1977. He is the legislator who
drafts new districts for the state of Massachusetts,
and is recognized as an able, honest, and respectable statesman.

Anne Avakian-Bishop of Los Angeles, California, noted
journalist, distinguished herself on the Bicentennial
Committee of the Los Angeles Press Council. Her
biography was included in the latest Who's Who In
America.

Haig Arakelian of San Diego, California, invented a
new tap-bug-proof telephone called Shield 100 and
produced by Aegis Electronics.

The Armenian Missionary Association of America (AMAA)
started publishing the AMAA News, which combines the
former A.M.A.A. Newletter and the Armenian American
Outlook.

The Armenian Library and Museum of America of Belmont, Massachusetts, has accumulated about 5,000
books on Armenian culture and heritage, mostly in
Armenian and English. The collection, which is
still in process of development, is considered one
of the most significant Armenian collections in the
United States. In addition, the institution has recently acquired a valuable collection of more than
100 Armenian coins, and several tape recording in-
terviews with elder Armenians from all over the
United States.

Levon Chaloukian of Los Angeles, California, purchased the Ryder Sound Services, Inc., and thus
became the   president and general manager of the
largest leading independent motion picture and
television sound recording company.

September. The first Armenian college in the United
States opened in La Verne, California. Twenty-nine
students enrolled Armenian courses for the first
semester, and will chose fields of specialization
in the following semesters.

Alice Keshishian started teaching a course on Armenia and Armenians at Harbor College, California.
The course includes language instruction, reading,
writing, speaking, and cultural history.

Michael Kermoyan, a well known stage and movie
actor, appeared in the role of a Russian military
judge in the NBC presentation called Francis Gary
Powers, the True Story of U-2 Spy Incidents.

November 5. The city of Stamford, Connecticut, paid
homage to Reuben Nakian, a noted sculptor, venerated
by art lovers in the United States and several countries. In the presence of the eighty year old celebrated sculptor, a slide program surveyed the artist's major works during the last five decades.

Under a grant from the Alex and Marie Manoogian
Foundation, the University of Michigan has intro-
duced a two-year program in the Armenian language.
The course is going to be taught by James Garabedian.

November 12. George Mardikian of San Francisco,
California, received the Horatio Alger Award, aimed
at encouraging young people to realize that success
in the United States can be achieved by any man or
woman regardless of race, creed, or origin.
Mardikian is the first Armenian American to be
honored with this award.

November 16. The Armenian Evangelical Church of
New York celebrated its eightieth anniversary of
its founding. Rev. Vartan Hartunian, pastor of the
First Armenian Church of Belmont, Massachusetts,
was the principal speaker.

November 26. More than 1,000 Armenian Americans,
many of whom came to this country during the last
few years, attended a meeting of solidarity with
Lebanese Armenians gravely affected by the civil

war between the Moslems and Christians of Lebanon.
The rally was held at St. Paul the Apostle Church
in New York City, and was addressed by numerous
Armenian American leaders.

An exhibit of water colors, oils and graphics by
Armenian American artists from the East Coast and
Canada was opened at the headquarters of the Ar-
menian General Benevolent Union, Inc. in New York
City.

November 28. A gala banquet, entitled "Thank You,
America" was held at the Hotel Waldorf Astoria in
New York City. The event was attended by 1,300
guests representing the Armenian American community
from coast-to-coast, and acknowledged the gratitude
the Armenian Americans foster towards the United
States, during the country's Bicentennial celebra-
tions.

Prominent Armenian American leaders led by Set C.
Momjian, chairman of the "Thank You, America" committee, presented a series of twenty-one tapestries
to the United States as a gift to the City of New
York. The tapestries, the work of Albert Herter,
depict different episodes in the history of New York
City during the last three centuries, and are deposited with the Metropolitan Museum of Art. On
this occasion, Mayor Abraham Beame declared November 28, 1976 as "Armenian, Thank You, America Day"
in New York City.

The Fourth Armenian Book Fair was held in Providence,
Rhode Island, under the auspices of the Knights of
Vartan, Arax Lodge. The fair presented 250 books in
English on Armenian history, culture, language, and
related subjects. The name of the fair was "Armenia:
It's Legacy to the World."

Thirty-one portraits in black and white and color,
by Christopher Der Manuelian of San Francisco, California, were selected by the Harvard University for
its Carpenter Visual Arts permanent collection.

December. William Saroyan's latest play Across the
Board on Tomorrow Morning was presented in Los
Angeles, California. Saroyan has also published
a new autobiographical work called Sons Come and
Go, Mothers Hang in Forever.

The Armenian Masons of Pennsylvania started prepar-
ations to celebrate the twenty-fifth anniversary of

the Ararat Square Club. The club has members representing Armenians belonging to different churches,
and has achieved a very strong fraternal and fellowship spirit. The actual celebration was scheduled
for March 1977, with the participation of Richard
S. Gulian, Grand Master of the Grand Lodge of New
Jersey. Mr. Gulian is the first Armenian American
to hold this honored position.

December 12. The 300th anniversary of the birth of
Mekhitar of Sebastia was celebrated in New York City
at the Hotel Statler-Hilton. The event was sponsored by six cultural associations, including the
Armenian Literary Society. Mekhitar (1676-1749)
was a Catholic priest, who promoted the idea of
uniting the Armenian Church with Rome. He built a
monastery on the Island of San Lazaro in Venice,
Italy, with a great library, and printing press.
The output of this press — Armenian religious,
language, literary, historical, scientific, and
other publications — played a very important role
in the development of the Armenian spiritual life
all over the world. Presently, the Mekhitarists,
a monastic congregation that follows the Benedectine
rule, has two centers: in Venice, Italy, and in
Vienna, Austria. Some Mekhitarists from Vienna,
Austria, staffed parishes in Cambridge, Massachusetts, and Los Angeles, California.

DOCUMENTS

THE ARMENIAN CAUSE DEBATED IN THE UNITED
STATES CONGRESS
1918

During World War I, when about 2,000,000
Armenians were massacred by Turkish authorities, the United States, embracing
the feelings of Armenian Americans,
strongly protested against the Turkish
atrocities, and opened the doors to
Armenian refugees to settle in America.
The situation of the Armenians in Turkey was debated by several Congresses
but became especially important after
May 25, 1918, when the Armenians who
survived the Turkish massacres, de-
feated an invading Turkish army, and
proclaimed and independent state called
The Republic of Armenia. The survival
and the recognition of the newly born
state within historical boundries became a vital issue for the Armenian
Americans and for the United States
foreign policy. The following is a
very good summary of the Armenian
cause brought to the attention of
the United States Senate by the Armenian National Delegation.

Source: U.S. Statutes at Large, 65th
Congress (1917-1918), 3rd Session,
Senate Document No. 316.

ARMENIA AND HER CLAIMS TO FREEDOM AND NATIONAL INDEPENDENCE.

Part I.

TURKISH ARMENIA AND THE ARMENIANS IN TURKEY.

We firmly believe that by her participation in the present world
war the United States will powerfully contribue toward cutting
the Gordian knot which goes by the name of the eastern question,
with the solution of which the fate of the Armenians is closely
bound up.

More than a century ago, Volney, an eminent French thinker and
philosopher, in an imperishable book, Les Ruines, heralded the ap-
proaching fall of the Ottoman Empire in these striking words: " The
hour of destiny has arrived; the catastrophe is about to commence."
He predicted the uprising of all the subject races of Turkey, including the Arabs, the Armenians and others, and his graphic

description of the condition of the Turkish Empire, the excesses of
the dominant Turk, the sufferings of the conquered races, and the
grievances of the latter against their " masters " were as true in an
aggravated form on the threshold of the present war as they were
when the great philosopher penned it.

Still the Ottoman Empire survived a century and its emascula-
tion has been gradual. This was chiefly due to the conflicting interests in the " great powers " of Europe in the East, to the political
credo prevailing in the chancellaries of Europe that the integrity
of the Ottoman Empire was essential for the maintenance of the
European equilibrium in the Near East, without which Turkey
would have been outlawed long ago and the several historic, progressive races comprising it emancipated from the yoke of a dominant
unspeakable military caste.

An empire that extended from the Caucasus to the Danube and
from the Bosporus to Carthage is reduced to a territory that comprises a strip of territory in Thrace, Asia Minor, Armenia, Syria,
and Palestine, Mesopotamia, and Arabia. In turn, Greece, Roumania, Montenegro, Serbia, and Bulgaria were emancipated from
Turkish domination. This gradual shrinkage should not be won-
dered at. The Turks conquered but never assimilated the progressive, historic, and civilized races of the Near East, whom they always
designated by the villifying name of Raia. By the very tenets, moreover, of Turkey's state doctrine, the conquered races were considered " flocks " which have been sent by the Almighty to be fleeced,
plundered, raped, and massacred whenever they protested against an
unspeakable tyranny.

We desire to remark here that Islamism, as understood and applied by the Turks, is not only as an author qualified it " a brain
disease," but it is also an essentially economic question. It is a sort
of league made up of all the Turkish elements that are unprepared
for the struggles of modern, strenuous life. They are all animated
by one identical belief, that they possess the unquestionable right to
be idle and that they are entitled to make the Armenians and other
conquered races work for them, since by their " divine " law these
are subjects reduced to a state of a " flock " to be fleeced.

This idea is the keynote of the whole eastern question.

Ever since western Europe, through an aberration of a political
mind, allowed in 1453 the Turks to supplant the cross by the crescent
at Constantinople the struggle in the Near East has been continuous
between progressive humanity on the one hand and obscurantism
and medieval barbarity on the other. There never has been a Turkish Government in the true sense of the word, a government such as
is conceived in western Europe or in the United States. " Massacre
and plunder " has been the invariable Turkish method of suppressing
complaints of the subject races or for despoiling them for the benefit
of the dominating race. The massacre of Chios in 1821, of Lebanon
in 1862, of Batak in 1876, and the appalling ruthless massacres of
Armenians of the Empire, extending from 1894 to 1896 and in 1909
and culminating in the deportations and extermination of the same
race in 1915 and thereafter, establish the veracity of this statement.

The expulsion of the Turks from Greece, Bulgaria, Serbia, Roumania, and from the Balkan Peninsula did not solve the near eastern
question in toto. There remain Arabia, Armenia, Egypt, and Palestine unredeemed.

The alliance between Prussian militarism and Turkish obscurantism
appears to keen observers a natural one. It is founded on a community of interest. Sultan Abdul Hamid inaugurated the understanding with the Kaiser so as to suppress more efficaciously all the
non-Turkish elements of the Empire and to counteract the reforming
spirit in the internal affairs of Turkey, with which the western powers
were animated for the purpose of upholding the " integrity " dogma

by strengthening the remaining conquered historic" races within the Empire.

This has been the dominant policy of the great powers since the Crimean power—a patchwork that crumbled as time proceeded, while it could not and did not modify Turkish mentality in the least.

The charter of Gulhane and of the Hatti Humayoum, issued through the "spontaneous good will" of the Sultan, and which claimed to place Christian and Turk on the same level and to secure to the former the elementary right that every citizen is entitled to possess—security of life, property, and honor—have remained a dead letter. Every bill of right conferred by the different Sultans during the nineteenth century on his Christian subjects has been preceded or followed by a recrudescence of persecution or massacres fomented and organized by the authorities. These were intended to be "manifestations" for the information of the European public against the recognition of civic rights to the subject races.

We need not rehearse here the whole sickening story of the unredeemed pledges of reform, which is admirably exposed in the work of Mr. Edward Engelhard, La Turque et le Tauzimat, where the French diplomatist and erudite conclusively establishes that "reforms" in Turkey were an exotic plant "adopted" by the Turkish statesmen so as to throw dust in the eyes of Europe, which was clamoring for them, and for the purpose of warding off an impending danger in the way of a European intervention.

The promulgation of the Turkish constitution of 1876—revived in 1908—has also been attributed to the same inherent causes, to the application of the same policy of prevarication, fraud, and make-beliefs as the events of the last 30 years have amply demonstrated. We need only recall that the Adana massacres of 1909, a year after the promulgation of the so-called Turkish constitution, were carried out by the soldiery under the command of Turkish officers, some of whom had obtained their military training in Germany.

While the Turkish rulers were, on the one hand, hoodwinking Europe with formal promises of reforms and with declarations conveying assurances regarding the betterment of the condition of the Christian populations of the Ottoman Empire, they were, on the other hand, systematically carrying on a policy of extermination of the non-Turkish elements. This has been especially so since the Paris treaty of 1856, which recognized the "integrity of the Ottoman Empire" as an essential article of international faith. When in 1862 the governor of Erzereum, Khaireddin Pasha, a Tunisian in the service of Turkey, reported to the Sublime Porte that the Armenians of Van, and Erzereum were emigrating in great numbers to escape the excesses of the Turkish officials, the depredations and acts of plunder committed by the Kurds and other predatory tribes, the grand vezir, Aali Pasha, the "great reformer," wrote back to instruct the governor "not to interfere in state affairs, that the Armenians can abandon their country and emigrate, as they will easily be supplanted by Mohammedan population from without."

To the policy of the extermination of non-Turks, Turkish statesmanship adhered to ever since with pertinacity until the war, when it considered this a favorable opportunity of giving it the finishing touch. We need only recall the awful story of the Armenian general massacres and deportations, the details of which are faithfully recorded in the archives of the State Department.

But we desire to throw a retrospective glance. In 1876, at the time of the Turco-Russian War, the grievances of the Armenians in Turkey may be summarized as follows:

1. The practical absence of political and civil equality.

2. The discrimination against non-Moslem evidence in the Turkish courts of justice.

3. The systematic pillage and destruction of Armenian villages, the sacking of Armenian public edifices, the perpetration of all kinds

of crimes and oppressive acts by the police, by officials, and by nomadic tribes aided and abetted in this by the authorities.

4. The venality of justice.

5. The systematic efforts to crush and ruin the peasant classes (1) by heavy taxes, (2) by expropriations, (3) by forcing them to abandon their holdings.

6. By forced conversion to Islam.

7. The systematic kidnapping of Armenian maidens and their incorporation in Turkish harems.

These were the elements that constituted the Armenian question. They are minutely set forth in numerous documents, in the reports of British consuls from 1840 to 1881, in the French Yellow Books, in the statement of travelers, and reliable and unbiased witnesses, and form an arsenal of facts and documents scientifically compiled in 1890 by Mr. Rolin Jacquemyns in his L'Armenie, les Armenians et le Traites, published in the Review of International Law of Bruxelles.

The Armenians hoped and waited and waited and hoped for the redress of their grievances by constant appeals to their " masters." The Turkish rulers instead of alleviating these bitter complaints, aggravated them and in truth none had been removed up to 1914, constitutions, bills of rights, and declarations to the contrary, notwithstanding.

The enmity of the Turk to commerce and civilization is easily demonstrated. Armenia by her industry, resources, and genius once supported a population of over 20,000,000, yet since it was brought under Turkish rule its natural resources remained undeveloped, pasture and arable lands were abandoned and falling out of cultivation, rivers choked up, roads broken, so that the country was fast becoming a dreary waste. To a similar pitiful condition were reduced the Balkan States. But since the Tartar foot departed from these countries even the most enthusiastic supporters of Turkey have been compelled to confess their admiration in many ways for these gallant little States.

Despairing of obtaining redress from their masters, the Armenians took occasion on the approach of the Russian Army to Constantinople in 1876 to appeal to Imperial Russia.

The treaty of San Stefano, in its article 16, makes special reference to the Armenians, and the treaty of Berlin, which substituted it, places the protection of the life, property, and honor of the Armenians under the collective control and guaranty of Europe.

The Anglo-Turkish convention of 1878, by which the administration of Cyprus was transferred to Great Britain, established a sort of British protectorate over Asia Minor, and while it resulted in the withdrawal of the Russians from Erzerum, it did not in any way benefit the Armenians. England ceased to send military consuls to Asia Minor in 1882 and the country was again exposed to the tender mercies of a hostile government. In a sense, the Berlin treaties and the Cyprus convention have done more harm than good. They raised hopes in the minds of the Armenians which were not realized, and the Turkish statesmen used every effort and strained every nerve to stamp these hopes out, either by exiling as many Armenians as they could from the soil of their ancestors or by fostering and encouraging Kurdish depredations, Circassian inroads, or by harassing religion and the schools.

The nomenclature of these outrages and misdeeds in Armenia are too long to be recited here, but the intolerable griefs and sufferings had culminated to such a point that the Armenians felt bound to appeal again to Europe by periodicals and publications in English and French or by sending deputations to Governments of the great powers, who had assumed the obligation of protecting this historic race. The Armenians were clearly realizing that unless drastic measures were taken by the concert of Europe they were doomed to extermination in the Ottoman Empire. Legitimate meetings, organized by the Armenians within the empire and without, were taken advantage of by Abdul Hamid to organize the general massacres of 1894 to 1896, the details of which are amply recorded in the official Blue Books and Yellow Books. After the massacres there was some hope of the introduction of positive reforms in the Armenian Provinces, but one of the greatest stumbling blocks for the realization of a reform program was the Government of Germany, who in return for a concession of a railway to Bagdad and other benefits, practically acquiesced in the policy of setting at naught the reforms intended to benefit not only the Armenian, but all the other inhabitants. The attempt made by England under Lord Salisbury to coerce the Turkish Government was also frustrated by the Government of the Czar. The diplomatic history of the last 30 years in connection with the solution of the Armenian question amply reveals that the Porte adroitly took advantage of the want of harmonious cooperation among the powers to play havoc with the Armenian population of Turkey for the purpose of creating a Turkey for the Turks exclusively. We need not refer in any detail to the so-called constitution of 1908, which was a snare and make-belief and which resulted in the Adana massacres, to which reference is given above, and to the deportations of a large section of the Armenian people during the year 1915 and thereafter, with the appalling and tragic results which have stirred the conscience of the civilized world.

PART II.

THE SITUATION OF THE ARMENIANS, INCLUDING TRANSCAUCASIA AND TURKEY, PRIOR TO THE PRESENT WORLD WAR.

When the present international war commenced, the number of Armenians living in the three Empires among which the country of Armenia is divided, viz, Russia, Turkey, and Persia, amounted to 4,276,000. Out of this number 3,406,000 inhabited on the soil of the historic land of Armenia, while the remaining 870,000 were scattered in different parts of the three Empires aforementioned. This circumstance demonstrates per se how the Armenian has tenaciously stuck to the land of his ancestors, notwithstanding the indisputable historic fact that no other nation on earth has undergone such vicissitudes and has shed so much of its precious blood for its national existence, ever since the fourth century anno Domini to the present day, during which long period it has become the standard bearer in the Near East—on the confines of Asia and Europe—of the ideas of civilization, liberty, and Christendom. Whereas other neighbors of the Armenians, who were exposed to the same fate, like the Jews and the Assyrians, do not present to-day the same conditions. The number of Israelites at present is more than 10,000,000 throughout the universe, but hardly 100,000 of these are on the soil of their historic fatherland; while the number of Assyrians, who in the distant past was computed by historians at about 30,000,000 souls, is at present reduced to hardly half a million survivors within the limits of the Ottoman Empire. But this number again has abandoned the land of its sires to find refuge in the mountains of Armenia and in the neighborly friendliness of the Armenians.

Let us now briefly set forth in what proportions the Armenians are located in the three Empires above referred to. The statistical information regarding the Armenians in Russian Armenia has been obtained from the official Russian census returns published in January of 1915, whereas what concerns the number of Armenians in Turkish Armenia are derived from the official archives of the Armenian Patriarchate of Constantinople prepared in 1912. The number of Armenians in Turkey in the year 1914 may be summed up as follows:

A. Within the limits of the country known as Turkish Armenia, the numbers are given against each of the Provinces that constitute the Armenian Provinces, to wit:

1. Vilayet of Erzereum	215,000
2. Vilayet of Van	185,000
3. Vilayet of Bitlis	180,000
4. Vilayet of Harpoot	168,000
5. Vilayet of Diarbekir	105,000
6. Vilayet of Sivas	165,000
7. Vilayet of Adana and Marash country, known as Cilicia	407,000
Total	1,425,000
Armenians inhabiting Constantinople, Smyrna, Thrace, and other parts of Turkish Empire	678,000
Grand total	2,103,000

B. Armenians in Russia in 1914:

1. Within the limits of Transcaucasia Province of Erivan	750,000
2. Elizabethpol	450,000
3. Tiflis	400,000
4. Kars	130,000
5. Bakou	128,000
	1,858,000
Northern part of the Caucasus and throughout Russia	150,000
Total	2,008,000

C. Armenians in Persia:

1. In the Province of Aderbeijan	120,000
2. In other parts of Persia	45,000
Total	165,000

From the above statistical returns it will be seen that no less than 3,403,000 Armenians were living on the soil of their fatherland on both sides of the Turco-Russian frontiers at the time when the present world war broke out. And by reason of her geographical position, Armenia became again the battle field of warring nations, and the Armenian people, faithful to their historic traditions and to their progressive past, at the very risk of their national existence, threw their lot on the side of the cause of justice and of civilization. The blood of the sons of Armenia was shed in torrents, in a way not commensurate with their numbers. Doubtless the historian of the future will record the indisputable fact that in this gigantic struggle among the warring nations, the smallest but the oldest of races, the Armenian, has proportionately offered greater sacrifices in blood on the altar of human liberty.

Before dilating upon the present claims of the Armenians, for the realization of which they have undergone such heavy sacrifices, may we be permitted to picture the conditions of the Armenian at the outlook of this war in the three empires between which Armenia is partitioned.

We will deal with each section separately.

Persian Armenia, which forms a part of the Persian Province of Aderbeijan, has been under Persian domination since the fifth century anno domini, although at different periods subsequent, it was united with the Armenian Kingdom of Van under the Arzrouni dynasty. The Armenians in Persian Armenia are the survivors of a much larger section of the race whose number has been depleted by reason of the successive conquests and raids of migratory tribes like the Tartars, Mongols, and Turks, that overran that part of the country in their successive onward marches toward the heart of Asia Minor. Notwithstanding the smallness of their number, the Armenians in Persia play a vital part in various walks of life. They have held important public offices; they have given statesmen, ambassadors, and military leaders to Persia; and the mercantile activity of that country with many quarters of the globe is in their hands. We may mention the names of the late Malcolm Han, ambassador to the Court of St. James; Nariman Han, ambassador to Vienna; Ohannes Han Masseghian, ambassador to Berlin, and others, who each and all were Armenians in the service of Persia. We think it is not out of place to recall the part played by Armenians in the reform and constitutional movement, one of whose principal leaders was an Armenian, Eprem Han and his associates, who were instrumental in introducing in the body politic of that Asiatic land the western ideas of progress and democracy and did not disdain to sacrifice their very lives for their realization.

In the fifth century, when the Persians were at the height of their power, they made attempts to impose on the Armenians by sheer violence their religious beliefs and compel them to forsake their national ideals. The struggle lasted about a century; and finding after protracted wars that it is impossible to make Armenians relinquish the tenets of their Christian faith and nationality, they altered their attitude and adopted a more tolerant policy toward them. For centuries ever since the Persians and Armenians have lived together as peaceful neighbors without the sanguinary conflicts which have characterized the Turco-Armenian relations since the Turkish conquest of part of Armenia. Although the Persiaas have mostly embraced Mohammedanism, but descending from an Aryan stock like the Armenians and being possessed of ancient culture and civilization, they have not displayed toward the Armenians the savagery and brutal conduct with which the Touranian races, to which the Turks belong, have familiarized the civilized world ever since they supplanted the cross by the crescent in the Near East.

Notwithstanding these somewhat bearable conditions prevailing in Persian Armenia—so contiguous to the Armenian Province of Van—the Armenians of Salmast, Khoi, and Makou, the principal Armenian-Persian centers in Aderbaijan, all aspire to see that part of their country one day united and form an inseparable part of a Magna Armenia.

Russian Armenia.—The part of historic Armenia which is under Russian sway is included in the Transcaucasian Provinces of Russia. It was conquered by the Russians in the early part of the nineteenth century and wrested from Persia. Before the Russian conquest Transcaucasia was divided between a number of Khanates and Melikates (small self-governing principalities). The Khans were Tartars by origin and ruled mostly over Tartars, while the Meliks were Armenian feudal lords, and their domination extended over the Armenian districts of Carabagh. All these different principalities were tributary to the Persian Government. Neighboring these dependencies to the northwest there existed a Georgian Kingdom, including the present Provinces of Tiflis and Kubias. Georgia, being squeezed in between two powerful Moslem countries like Persia and Turkey, and subject to permanent attacks from these quarters, appealed, toward the end of the eighteenth century, to the Empress Catherine for protection and help. At this juncture, in the year 1787, the Armenian Meliks of Carabagh took occasion to send a delegation to the Russian court praying for Russian assistance against Tartar neighbors, who were in constant conflict with them. The Russian Government promised immediate help to both Armenians and Georgians, and, moreover, undertook, in so far as the Armenians were concerned, to free them from Persian domination and to organize a new Armenian State made up of the Armenian Provinces under the suzerainty of Russia.

Encouraged by these promises, both Armenians and Georgians placed all their military forces at the disposal of Russia and powerfully contributed to bring about the conquest of Transcaucasia from

Persia. But, unfortunately, the solemn promises of the Empress Catherine were not fulfilled and the conquered territory was brought under Russian sway. It was through the enforcement of this method that Georgia and part of historic Armenia, including Echmadzin, the seat of the supreme head of the Armenia church and nation, were annexed by Russia.

The policy of Russia ever since these conquests appears to have had a single purpose, viz, to Russianize and assimilate the Armenians and Georgians. The Georgians, being members of the Eastern Greek Church, and hence of the same religious denomination as the Russian, were more easily amenable to Russification than were the Armenians, who, having a national separate church of their own, were more jealous of their national traditions. This circumstance provoked the enmity of the Russian Government toward them. The policy of Russification was strengthened more and more, and in 1903 the Armenian schools were closed and all national Armenian property confiscated by an imperial ukase issued by the now deposed Emperor Nicholas II. The Armenians did not, however, willingly submit to these arbitrary acts and opposed violence to violence, and in certain sections of the Transcaucasus several Armenians were killed by Russian soldiers. The illustrious Khrimian, the Catholicos of all Armenians and the idol of the nation, scorning exile to Siberia at the age of 80, in an historic document addressed to the Omnipotent Czar of All Russia, declared that he, as the custodian of the centuries-old heritage of the Armenian Nation, refused to abide by such an unjust decree. As a result, the prisons in the Transcaucasus were filled with hundreds of Armenians, and many others belonging to the intellectual classes were exiled to Siberia. But the Russian administration did not rest here. It went further. It incited the Tartars of the Transcaucasus against the Armenians. It distributed firearms among the Tartars of Bakou and Elizabethpol and gave them carte blanche to plunder ind kill their Armenian neighbors, and organized pogroms as it did with Russian Jews.

In February, 1905, the Tartars of Baku and elsewhere began their unprovoked onslaught on the Armenians under the very eyes of the Russian police, who remained passive observers f these sanguinary scenes. These attacks were extended suddenly to other centers like

Elizabethpol, Shoushi, Eriven, and Nakhitehan, and took the Armenians by surprise. The Armenians were aware that the reactionary policy of Russia, which had prevailed since the advent to the throne of Emperor Alexander III, was anti-Armenian in its essence. They also knew that after the general massacres of the Armenians in Turkey in 1895 and 1896, Count Lebanoff, the Russian foreign minister, declared Russia was eager to have Turkish Armenia, but without the Armenians, whom he did not care to save. All these circumstances notwithstanding, the Armenians in Russia could never imagine that a Christian power like Russia would countenance and authorize the Mohammedan element in the Transcaucasus to assume a hostile attitude toward them. But the facts were staring the Armenians in the face. There was no time to lose. They at once organized themselves for self-defense and Transcaucasia became the theater of a civil war between these two elements which lasted a whole year under the very eyes of the Russian authorities, who only interfered when they realized that the Tartars were being worsted by the Armenians. The Armenians lost 1,556, while the loss of the Tartars during these frays amounted to 5,635 men, and this disproportion of the fallen is due to the admirable organization of the Armenians, who, notwithstanding their being somewhat numerically inferior to their assailants, were able on the spur of the moment to organize their forces for self-defense. But the material injuries inflicted on the Armenians were much greater than those borne by the Tartars.

It would, however, be fair to state here that, notwithstanding the

Russian bureaucratic methods of government and all its deficiencies and its hostile policy toward the Armenians, the latter nevertheless enforced in the Transcaucasus certain elementary rights of existence of which they have ever been deprived in Turkey—which enabled them to develop their moral and material resources, to increase in numbers, and to become the most forward element of the Transcaucasus in all the branches of human activity. In proof of this we desire to recall that in 1836 the number of Armenians under Russian domination amounted to about 300,000 as against 500,000 Georgians and 700,000 Tartars. In 1915, according to official statistics, the number of Armenians swelled to 1,858,000, that of the Georgians to 1,450,000, and of the Tartars to 2,040,000. The large increase of Armenians may be also explained by the influx of Armenian refugees from Turkey; but the real cause of this increase is due principally to the fact that the Armenians are a prolific race, with strong family virtues. The official Russian statistics demonstrate that the rate of increase per year of these different races is as follows:

Per cent.

Armenians _____ 2.5
Georgians _____ 1.5
Tartars _____ .9

We can not close this chapter without alluding to the intellectual and cultural progress of the Armenians under Russia. There in the Transcaucasus throve in a marked degree Armenian literature which produced a galaxy of writers, poets, novelists, historians, whose writings are to some degree permeated with the ideas of the most liberal Russian leaders of thought. These ideas in return brought to bear the weight of their influence on the minds of their Armenian compatriots across the border into Turkish Armenia, toward whose struggles for emancipation from the Turkish yoke the Armenians of Russia greatly contributed.

When the present war broke out the Armenians of Russia forgot for a moment all the just complaints against Russian bureaucracy and, without hesitation or equivocation, espoused the cause of the allies, including Russia, with the firm conviction that the victory of the allies would end their sufferings and would recognize their inalienable rights to self-government. Besides contributing 160,000 men to the Rusisan Army, they organized several volunteer corps, whose deeds of valor on the battlefield were officially recognized by M. Sazanoff, the foreign minister, in his address to the Duma.

Without the contribution of the Armenian contingents to the Russian Army in the Caucasus the Turkish offensive against the Transcaucasus in 1914 and 1915 would have been crowned with success, more especially having regard to the fact that the sympathies of the Tartar and Georgian population of the Transcaucasus were manifestly pro-Teutonic and pro-Turk. The success of such an offensive in the years 1914 and 1915 would have enabled the Turkish armies to secure a footing at Baku, and all its oil wells and Persian Afghanistan—the gates to India—would have been placed at the mercy of the Germanic-Turkish forces. This active participation of the Russian Armenians at this crucial phase of the world war was publicly recognized by the Young Turk leaders, who invoked this circumstance to justify the Turkish savageries perpetrated against the Armenians of Turkey.

Let it be said, moreover, that after the disruption of Russia, through the triumph of bolshevism and the withdrawal of the Russian troops from the Caucasian front in January, 1918, it was the Armenian contingents solely that held the line against the Turkish onslaughts and thereby helped the Mesopotamian wing of the British Army by preventing the Turkish troops on the Caucasian front from joining the Turkish armies operating against the British. The Armenians held the line until September, 1918, and it was after hard-fought battles that the Turks were able to reach Baku, the

British expeditionary force sent to join hands with them not arriving in due time, and those that did arrive were insufficient in numbers.

These services have been officially acknowledged in official dispatches by the British Government, and we take occasion to reproduce the following extract from a letter, dated the 3d of October, 1918, signed by the undersecretary of state, Robert Cecil, and addressed to Lord James Bryce:

The Baku Armenians were not only an isolated remnant, but no doubt their task was made impossible from the outset by the disorganization which prevailed and had thrown open to the Turks the Transcaucasian Railway leading to the gates of the city. Whatever may have happened at Baku, the responsibility can not be laid at the door of the Armenian people.

The national delegation, commissioned by his holiness the Katholikos in 1913 to obtain from the civilized world that justice to Armenia which has been delayed with such terrible consequences, have given many proofs, under the distinguished presidency of his excellency Boghos Nubar Pasha, of their devotion to the cause of the allies as being the cause of all peoples striving to free the world from oppression.

The council at Erivan threw itself into the breach which the Russian breakdown left open in Asia, and after organizing resistance to the Turks in the Caucasus from February to June this year was at length compelled by main force to suspend hostilities. Great Britain and her allies understand the cruel necessity which has forced the Armenians to take this step and look forward to the time, perhaps not far distant, when allied victories may reverse their undeserved misfortunes.

Meanwhile, the services of the Armenians to the common cause, to which you refer in your letter, have assuredly not been forgotten; and I venture to mention four points which the Armenians may, I think, regard as the charter of their right to liberation at the hand of the allies:

(1) In the autumn of 1914 the Turks sent emissaries to the national congress of the Ottoman Armenians, then sitting at Erzerum, and made them offers of autonomy if they would actively assist Turkey in the war. The Armenians replied that they would do their duty individually as Ottoman subjects, but that as a nation they could not work for the cause of Turkey and her allies.

(2) On account, in part, of this courageous refusal the Ottoman Armenians were systematically murdered by the Turkish Government in 1915. Two-thirds of the population were exterminated by the most cold-blooded and fiendish methods—more than 700,000 people—men, women, and children alike.

(3) From the beginning of the war that half of the Armenian Nation which was under the sovereignty of Russia organized volunteer forces and, under their heroic leader, Andranik, bore the brunt of some of the heaviest fighting in the Caucasian campaigns.

(4) After the breakdown of the Russian Army at the end of last year these Armenian forces took over the Caucasian front and for five months delayed the advance of the Turks, thus rendering an important service to the British Army in Mesopotamia. These operations in the region of Alexandropol and Erivan were, of course, unconnected with those at Baku.

I may add that Armenian soldiers are still fighting in the ranks of the allied forces in Syria. They are to be found serving alike in the British, French, and American armies, and they have borne their part in Gen. Allenby's great victory in Palestine.

From the above-mentioned uncontrovertible facts it is conclusively established that the Armenians from the beginning of the war, and notwithstanding the justifiable mistrust which they have maintained toward the aims of Russian imperialism, have stood by and been loyal to the allied cause in the Near East, and they rendered not only appreciable military service but also jeopardized their very existence in Turkey, where more than a million of Armenians, men, women, and children, were ruthlessly massacred and exterminated by reason of their proally attitude.

PART III.

WHAT ARE THE CLAIMS OF THE ARMENIANS?

Having regard to the historic past of the Armenians, and to the fact that even at present they constitute the most civilized and progressive and producing elements in the environments in which they live, they expect their final deliverance as the result of the present war.

As before stated, half of the Armenian population inhabited within the limits of Russian Transcaucasia, while the other half, numbering about 2,100,000, were in Turkey. Faithful to its past methods, the Turkish Government, taking advantage of the opportunities presented by the present war, attempted to solve the Armenian question by exterminating that part of the Armenian population which was in a majority within the frontiers of its historic fatherland.

It is estimated that the number of Armenians slaughtered in 1915 by the agents of the Turkish Government amounted to from 600,000 to 1,000,000. Let us suppose for a moment that not a single Armenian out of the 2,100,000 has escaped the hands of the Turkish executioner. We claim that however reduced the number of Armenians may be to-day their homelands of 1914 should belong to the survivors.

According to laws of all civilized people, including the Sheri law, no murderer can inherit the property of the victim of his crime. That inheritance or estate must pass not to the murderer but to the next of kin of the victim.

We leave to the future to determine the exact number of Armenian victims as the result of the massacres and so-called deportations of 1915. We are not, however, far from the truth in asserting that at least 1,000,000 Armenians have been saved out of the 2,100,000 Armenians who inhabited Turkish Armenia in 1914. This million of survivors includes the 300,000 Aremenians who have sought refuge in the Transcaucasus, as also about 200,000 Armenians who have migrated to America, Egypt, and Europe.

To this million must be added the 2,000,000 Armenians of the Transcaucasus. These 3,000,000 Armenians are those who can lay claim to the heritage of which the present Turkish Government has attempted to deprive them by methods known to all.

The Armenian people venture to hope that this appalling crime is going to be the last act in the sanguinary history of the Ottoman Empire, which has for the last five centuries exposed to ruin and desolation and massacre the cradles of civilization and religion. It is impossible to conceive that the present civilized world will permit a race with such a criminal record and government to continue unrestrained and unpunished to exterminate peoples superior to it in culture and usefulness, such as the Armenians, the Greeks, the Arabs, and the Jews.

The complete liquidation of the Ottoman Empire should be involved, and it will be incumbent on the Areopagus of nations to handle the same at the coming peace congress. together with the solution of the Armenian question. The dissolution of the Ottoman Empire should have been brought about a century ago, soon after the Greek war of independence, and mankind would thereby have been spared much innocent blood. We are convinced that the participation of the United States in the present war will be instrumental in bringing about a solution of the near eastern and Armenian questions, not by the methods of an antiquated European diplomacy, but in a spirit of fair play to satisfy the just claims of the various long-suffering people of the Near East concerned.

Before dealing with the Armenian question let us be permitted to submit the produs procedendi. which in our opinion must be followed in order to insure a radical and equitable solution of the entire near eastern problem.

The allies have on many occasions proclaimed the right of nations to self-determination. On the basis of this fundamental principle, the peoples and races inhabiting the Ottoman Empire are entitled to receive from that morally and materially bankrupt State a territory as their share proportionate to the numbers which each of them had prior to 1914, and not according to the respective number of their present depleted populations, for the simple reason that human conscience can not in any way sanction the murders and forced deportations premeditated and carried into effect by the Turkish Government for the purpose of " reducing " the number of the non-Turkish population of the Empire. It follows that if 500,000 Armenians

have survived out of a population of 2,100,000 the former are fully
entitled to such territory as should be allotted to the 2,100,000 Armenians who were in existence in 1914. Otherwise we would be
putting a premium on crime.

Let us now consider which are, in their respective numbers, the
populations composing the Turkish Empire, and in what way or
manner can satisfaction be given to its different elements on historical
and ethnological grounds.

After the Balkan War the Turkish Government held sway over
a territory covering an area of about 1,800,000 square kilometers in
round figures. This area does not include the deserts of Mesopotamia
and Arabia, but only the inhabited territories which constituted the
Ottoman Empire "Vilayets" (Provinces).

In this immense territory of 1,800,000 square kilometers, which
covers an area about four times the size of France, was a population
of between eighteen and twenty millions. Armenia, alone, in the past,
as history tells us, had a prosperous population of 26,000,000, whereas
Mesopotamia, now with hardly 806,000 inhabitants, had in the distant past 28,000,000 souls. These 18,000,000 of inhabitants were
made up approximately as follows:

Arabs (including Syrians)	5, 900, 000
Armenians	2, 100, 000
Greeks	1, 800, 000
Other Christian races	1, 200, 000
Kurds	700, 000
Kizilbaches	500, 000
Jews	400, 000
Non-Turkish races	12, 600, 000
Turks	5, 400, 000
Total	18, 000, 000

These 5,400,000 Turks comprise Circassian and Mahommedan tribes
who have migrated from the Caucasus into Asia Minor, and whose
number is about 300,000, as also some other minor races whose origin
is not Turkish and whose religion is not Mohammedan but whose
vernacular is Turkish, like the Tahtadji tribes in the Cilician regions.

The inference to be drawn from these figures is that the Turks, who
are the dominant race in the Empire, constitute one-third of the
entire population, a minority who prey on a majority. There was a
time when the Turkish race, or rather the military caste that goes
under this name, did not represent even the one-twentieth, nay, the
one-hundredth of the entire population of the Empire. This was
five centuries prior, when the limits of the Empire extended from the
Persian Gulf to Algeria and from the outskirts of Vienna to Egypt
in the south.

In this phase of Turkish history the " subject " races were compara-
tively much less exposed to exploitation by having to " feed " their
then masters than they are now when it is computed that every two
non-Turks—subjects of the Empire—have to feed and maintain one
parasite Turk. This is one of the secrets of the decay of the Ottoman Empire.

Let us now consider how the national claims of Armenia should be
adjusted and the national aspirations realized. Armenian territory
in Turkey includes the six Armenian vilayets and the Province of
Cilicia, in accordance with the solemn declaration contained in
diplomatic documents of the six great powers of Europe.

The areas covered by these administrative divisions are as follows:

	Square kilometers.
Vilayet of Erzereum	49, 700
Vilayet of Bitlis	27, 100
Vilayet of Van	39, 300
Vilayet of Harpoot	32, 900
Vilayet of Diarbekir	37, 500
Vilayet of Sivas	62, 100

Vilayet of Adana	39,900
District of Marash	20,000
Total	308,500

The Turkish Government, so far back as 1878, anticipating the "Armenian danger," arbitrarily modified the limits of the Armenian Provinces, with a view to swelling the numbers of Moslems and making it appear that the Turks are in a majority. Thus the frontiers of Sivas and Diarbekir and Adana were enlarged so as to include regions not inhabited by Armenians. If we are to sever from the above three vilayets those portions which have been artificially added to the original provincial delimitations, we obtain a total approximate area of 220,000 square kilometers, wherein the Armenian element was in the majority in the year of 1914.

The following is the return of the populations inhabiting Armenia, presented by the Armenian Patriarchate in 1912 to ambassadors of the great powers at Constantinople when the question of Armenian reforms was again on the tapis in 1912:

Armenians	1,425,000
Assyrians	123,000
Kizilbashes	220,000
Yezidis	37,000
Mahommendau Kurds	424,000
Turks	871,000
Total	3,100,000

The Armenians represented 46 per cent, the Turks 28 per cent, the Kurds 13.7 per cent, of the population of the said Provinces, while the remaining percentage of 12.3 per cent was made up of non-Turkish or non-Mahommedan elements. It was with a view to modifying this proportion of numbers that the Ottoman Government for the last 40 years has had recourse to periodical massacres culminating in the 1915 tragic events. By disposing of the Armenians, Turkish statesmen considered they were getting rid of the Armenian question once for all.

To sum up, the Armenians are fully entitled, according to their numbers, on historical, geographical, and ethnological grounds, to a territory covering an area of 280,000 square kilometers, extending from the Gulf of Alexandretta (known as Sea of Armenia in medieval times) to the Russo-Persian frontier. We shall deal separately with the natural boundaries of the territory in question. We now propose to deal with the Turkish race.

Excluding Syria, Mesopotamia, Kurdistan, Armenia, and Arabia, the remaining vilayets of Turkey and central and western Asia Minor are the folowing:

	Square kilometer.
European Turkey	26,100
District of Ismidt	8,100
District of Bigha	6,600
Vilayet of Brussa	65,800
Vilayet of Smyrna	55,300
Vilayet of Konia	102,100
Vilayet of Angora	70,900
Vilayet of Kastamouni	50,700
Vilayet of Trebizonde	32,400
Total	418,000

Add to these numbers 50,000 square kilometers for the non-Armenian regions comprised in the vilayets of Sivas and Adana and we get a total of 468,000 square kilometers of territory left for the future Turkish State; but whereas out of the above territory a slice of land of the Black Sea should be made part of future Armenia in order that she may have an outlet to the sea, and after disposing of the Greek claims in Ionia, there still remain about 400,000 square kilometers in Anatolia for the future Turkish State, which will con-

tain what remains of the Turkish element, aggregating to something
like 4,000,000 people.

This solution of the eastern question would not be, we admit,
palatable to the present rulers of Turkey, but the plain Turkish
people would welcome it. It insures their future interests in an
appreciable manner and is preferable to the uncertainty of their
present condition. It has other advantages. A Turkish State without "subject" races may be an incentive to the Turks to radically
modify their modes of living, to cease becoming parasites, and thus
earn their daily bread with the sweat of their brows. They may
thereby gradually enter the family of civilized nations.

But it is opportune to recall that by reason of the destruction of
Russia and Russian imperialism, and having regard to the newly
accepted doctrine of self-determination for nations, it is but fair and
just that a one and indivisible Armenia, including Russian, Persian,
and Turkish Armenia, should be constituted as one independent
State. In part of this memorandum we mentioned that there are
1,856,000 Armenians in the Transcaucasus bordering Turkish Armenia. It would be natural to unite the fractions torn asunder of the
Armenian Nation so as to constitute a Magna Armenia made up of
Russian, Persian, and Turkish Armenia. The Transcaucasian Provinces, where the Armenians are in a majority, are the following:

	Square kilometers.	Population.
1. Province of Erivan	27,777	750,000
2. Province of Kars	18,749	130,000
3. Mountainous district of Elizabethpol	22,000	450,000
Total	68,526	1,330,000

Interspersed among this Armenian population there are 545,000
Mahommedans, Tartars, and Turks, while there are about 526,000
Armenians scattered in the Georgian and the Tartar Provinces of
Transcaucasia. This proximity offers great facilities to these dif-
ferent elements to settle on the respective territories to be allotted to
them by the peace congress as a result of this world war.

To summarize, the future Armenian State may therefore include:

	Square kilometers.
Turkish Armenia	220,000
Russian Armenia	68,526
Persian Armenia	15,000
Total	303,526

In our opinion, the aforementioned should be the boundaries and
extent of the future Armenian State. The State thus created should
be able to develop economically in a normal fashion and without
hindrance, and it will, moreover, be in a position to fulfill its political
and civilizing mission and become the corner stone of a lasting peace
in the Near East, with a population of 3,000,000 Armenians and
with about one million to one million and a half non-Armenian
elements.

Part IV.

WHAT INTEREST HAVE THE ALLIES IN CREATING AN INDEPENDENT ARMENIA?

We venture to state that an Armenia created under these conditions, whose freedom and independence shall be guaranteed by all the
powers and by a league of nations, will in the Near East play the part
that Switzerland does in Europe. By reason of her geographical
position, Armenia is more important than Switzerland, which stands
between four European powers, two of which belong to the Latin and
the other two to the Teutonic races. Whereas the Armenian plateau,
which covers an extensive area between the Black and Mediterranean

Seas, by the very nature of its exceptional position will not only stand between Georgia, Turkey, Syria, the Tartar regions of the Caucasus, Persia, Mesopotamia, and Kurdistan, namely, seven different States, but being so situated that it has almost become the converging point of Europe, Asia, and Africa, is destined also to become the land where all races may intermingle and diverge. This is a vital consideration which requires that a land so situated should be neutralized so that no Government or people should in any way be able to utilize it for purposes of conquest, as has happened so often in the past. This in itself is a vital reason for the creation of an Armenia, destined to insure the equilibrium in the Near East.

The immediate services such a State can render will be to obstruct the "drang nach Osten" policy of Germany by neutralizing the Berlin-Bagdad line that runs through Armenia. Another salutary consequence of the creation of such a State would be to arrest the Young Turkey's panaslamic and pantouranian aggressive movement and to build up a barrier against it. Although the pantouranian movement is in its infancy at present, we can not disregard its future potentialities and measures ought to be taken to arrest its baneful effects, otherwise, it may become as dangerous an element for the future of mankind as is Pan Germanism at present, having, moreover, in view the circumstance that the center of this pantouranian movement would be in Berlin and not Constantinople and exploited by Germany for the purpose of furthering her designs of domination and aggrandizement. Besides these two aggressive movements, there may be danger in the future that Imperial Russia, after traversing this present phase of dissolution, may emerge triumphant, and in such a circumstance, a neutralized Armenia would be the only barrier to be opposed to a possible aggressive Russia.

The above political circumstances do not stand alone. There is another higher justification which renders imperative the restoration of Armenia to freedom, and this is in the supreme interests of civilization. We all know that the enlightened countries of the west have inherited their culture from those ancient peoples of the Near East. Under the scimitar of the Turks, it has been buried for centuries and was threatened with eternal decay. It is high time to restore to the east that share of light and progress of which it became the cradle and the principal source. To accomplish this, the democratic nations of the earth have a duty to perform toward the Armenian people, by bringing about their emancipation and insuring their existence against final extinction, in order that a people susceptible of the highest culture may be able to fulfill its glorious civilizing mission in the Near East.

All the European savants are of the unanimous opinion—and in this the German professors concur—that the Armenian represents the only element in the Near East that can play the part of the intermediary between the eastern and western world. The Turk, the Arab, the Georgian, the Kurd, or the Persian, who are his neighbors, do not possess the aptitudes to disseminate European and American civilization as does the Armenian. Ethnologists are all agreed in stating that the Armenians, being a branch of the Indo-European race, settled on the Armenian plateau 27 centuries ago, while they embraced Christianity as far back as the fourth century, and ever since have kept aloft the ideas of Christian thought and civilization against the onslaught of semisavage Asiatic and Mohammedan races. The experience they have acquired of a life replete with vicissitudes and tribulations in their contact with the eastern nations has developed in them extraordinary qualities such as no other people possess. If the times are ripe in order that the different parts of humanity should be brought more closely in touch with each other, so that they may come to an understanding and to create more decent relations among them, it is the Armenian who is destined to become the connecting link between Christianity and Asia.

CONCLUSION.

After unprecedented vicissitudes and tribulations, the Armenians claim a fitting place in the concert of free and independent nations. Armenia, like Poland, claims to be one and indivisible, and the future Armenian State should by right include Russian, Persian, and Turkish Armenia—from the Caucasus to the Straits of Alexandretta. To this territory Armenia is entitled on historical and ethnological grounds, and it is indispensable that the Cilician Provinces of Armenia bordering on the Gulf of Alexandretta should be included in Armenia Irredenta. Cilicia was an independent State at the end of the fourteenth century. Therein is situated Adana, where the massacres of 1909 took place, and there, in the fastnesses of the Taurus, the Armenians held their own against Turkish barbarism for centuries, and in the course of the nineteenth century fought heroically against overwhelming Turkish armies.

The Armenians do not claim any territory which is not their own, nor is it fair that they should accept any solution which does not vouchsafe to them an independence such as Greece, Serbia, and Roumania possess. Massacres and deportations do not constitute rights for the Turkish executioners of the Armenian race. The number of Armenians has been reduced by reason of these atrocities, but there are at least 3,000,000 survivors of the Armenian holocaust who are entitled to the territory claimed. Greece at the time of her emancipation, in 1829, hardly contained half a million people. Notwithstanding, Europe recognized Greek independence after the Battle of Nefarino, which sealed the death of Turkish domination in Hellas, whose population has now more than quadrupled. It will be the same of Armenia if she be allowed to develop and breathe freely as a sovereign independent State. The thirteen States of America that revolted against Great Britain at the time of their liberation did not contain more than 4,000,000 people, and they covered a territory far greater in extent than would the future Armenian State. The argument that the Armenian population has been depleted is a very loose one. To accept the same and to make it weigh in the balance against Armenian claims would be to put a premium on crime and to legitimatize the massacres and deportations carried out by the Turks during these last 30 years, culminating in the events of 1915 and 1916, to which reference is made in the first part of this memorandum.

And let us record here that Armenia, by reason of her civilization in the east, her immeasurable sacrifices, especially her military assistance to the allied cause, in the Caucasus, in Palestine, and in France, to which expression is given in the correspondence exchanged between Lord Cecil and Lord Bryce, referred to in this memorandum, is entitled to complete restoration of her national independence. Through the ages her spiritual and patriotic leaders have kept alive and alight the flame of national consciousness and self-government, despite successive dominations and persecutions. Her political and military struggles against Turkish barbarism during the last 30 years are admirable credentials for her to present to the future peace congress.

The founding of the diminutive Republic of Ararat is a small beginning for national government for the whole of Armenia, from the Caucasus, through Cilicia, to the Mediterranean. Any scheme which may be advocated by certain elements in this country having for their object to preserve Turkey as a unit are of a nature to defeat the imperishable rights of the Armenians to freedom and independence. Such schemes are, moreover, detrimental to the cause of the allies and to the United States, and unworthy of the noble traditions bequeathed by the founders and continuators of this great Republic.

To sum up, Armenia is Europe and America is Asia in the bud. Let western civilization take care of it. It is a bud out of which will develop fresh elements of æsthetic, moral, and spiritual progress.

The Armenian race, by its strong national, religious, and philosophical turn of mind, is the equal of all the fine, sensitive natures among the peoples of Europe and America. Her cause therefore appeals strongly to every State and people, all of whom should agree to grant to Armenia that which she wants and demands at the close of this great war; namely, complete freedom and national independence.

SURVEY OF ARMENIAN AMERICANS
1919

The following is the first survey on
Armenian Americans, prepared as a
lesson in Americanism, and especially
designed for school use.

Source: Literary Digest, (January 4,
1919)

WHY THE ARMENIANS CAME HERE—In every case
of the immigration of a foreign people to these
shores there will be found specific reasons for the
movement. The Armenians came as the result of two very
different impulses: They were tyrannized by the "unspeakable Turk"; and they were educated by Christian missionaries. Now there is an estimated Armenian population here of
seventy-five to one hundred thousand, the majority of whom
settled here after the massacres of 1895–1896. Yet as long
ago as 1860 various individual Armenians ventured into this
country for educational and commercial purposes.

The original Armenian merchant in the United States appeared shortly after the Crimean War and engaged in the
business of exporting American agricultural implements to
Turkey. Later his promotive genius led him to draw a number
of his countrymen to Fresno County, California, where they
busied themselves with agricultural pursuits, including vine-
yards, orchards, truck-farming, and the like. This agricultural
colony of Armenians in California has flourished to this day, and
one member of it, because of his success in raising and selling
melons, is generally known as "The Melon King."

WHERE ARMENIANS CONGREGATE — The greater part
of our Armenian population is established on the Atlantic and
on the Pacific seaboard. Scattering units of about 20,000
dwell and work in the inland sections. In the East they are
most numerous in Boston and cities of the vicinage. Then we
find great numbers in New York City and in Providence and
adjacent towns, in Troy, Philadelphia, and West Hoboken.
A considerable Armenian population is to be found also in
Chicago. Generally speaking, Armenians do not cluster in
colonies in these cities but live in various parts so that we never
hear of a "Little Armenia."

THEIR OCCUPATIONS—In all centers of Armenian distribution the professions are adequately represented. We have
Armenian physicians, lawyers, clergymen, journalists, authors,
and dentists. In commerce some of the best-known men are
rug merchants, not only importers but also manufacturers of a
domestic product in rug-weaving. For a certain period, approximately until about ten years ago, Armenian merchants
practically controlled the importation of oriental rugs. In the
larger cities many Armenians make their way as tradesmen
and shopkeepers, while in centers of mechanical industry, such as
Detroit, many are to be met as workers in factories. Some
are employed in the less technical branches of manufacture, but
there are many also whose skill is devoted to the finer work of
machine and tool construction. In cities such as Worcester
(Mass.), Providence, Troy, Cleveland, and Detroit perhaps
60 to 65 per cent. of the Armenians are employed in factories.
The problem of the abandoned farms of New England was met
to a limited degree in Maine, New Hampshire, Massachusetts,
and Rhode Island by Armenians, who went in courageously
for truck-farming. Yet we are told that the short seasons of

planting and reaping, owing to climatic conditions, inclines them to the more favorable agricultural zones of the Pacific Coast and elsewhere. As one Armenian farmer in New England exprest it, "I have only three really good months to work in."

WHAT THEY GET AND GIVE OUT OF THE DAY'S WORK —The first half of this indirect question may be most briefly answered by the statement of a prominent American citizen of Armenian birth that the Armenians are "in the main prosperous" in all classes. To reply to the second part, it is to be noted that no matter how Armenians may thrive here they have always in mind the terror and misery "over there" at the hands of the "unspeakable Turk." For the aid given by Americans, of all sorts and conditions, Armenians here have only gratitude and praise. At the same time Armenians themselves are ever mindful of their families, relatives, and friends in their distrest country. After the massacres of 1895–96 the Armenian Benevolent Association was organized in Egypt to help Armenians remaining in the homeland by supplying villages with schools, orphanages, with live stock, and agricultural implements. All such succor had to be given secretly because of the Turkish domination. For some years the contributions through this organization averaged $15,000 per year. The Armenian is rare who is not a member of this society and the subscriptions range from $3 a year—or 25 cents per month—upward. Through exceptional effort in 1916 the association sent abroad $300,000; in 1917 $500,000, in the past year $1,000,000. The explanation for this is simple. Apart from the ruination of land and industry by the Turks some Armenians have lost by massacre or privation from ten to fifteen members of their family and relatives.

HOW ARMENIANS TAKE ROOT HERE—Seven thousand miles away by perilous journey of rail and water lies Armenia, from which many natives escaped as proscribed citizens. Married men with their families incline rapidly to become naturalized and settle here for good. Single men, especially those of the age of nineteen or over whose occupation does not easily permit them to learn English, are disposed to go back to rejoin their families or to marry a wife they can understand when she talks. Nevertheless, many bring their wives back to this country and others return because they have learned to love the freedom and comforts of life in the United States. Many Armenians go back home to protect their property interests or those of their family and relatives.

LITERACY AND EDUCATION—The percentage of literacy among the Armenians is much higher than among some other immigrant races. Judged by the Armenian language, the percentage of literates is more than 90 per cent., and judged by the English language it is estimated at 60 per cent. Armenian children are brought up in the public schools, and it is to be noted that a goodly proportion of them follow on through high school, where their rating is good. The children are naturally bilingual, tho, as has been the case with other races, they incline to talk English in preference to their mother tongue because of their associations away from home. Oddly enough the parents, in their contact with the children, incline to pick up English words and phrases, so that intercourse sometimes becomes spotted with quaint Armenian-English combinations of expression. The literacy rating of the Armenians is not to be surprised at, because they are known as a studious race. Not a few who have passed the age of school days and are employed in working hours acquire an American education by attending night school. There is record of one Armenian who, at the age of seventy, went to night school to learn English. As another cultural influence, we are told that nearly every Armenian family here reads one or two Armenian papers, of which there are two dailies, several weeklies, some biweeklies, and a few monthly magazines.

RELIGION—It has been said above that one of the factors in Armenian immigration has been education by Christian missionaries. To-day there are more than fifty Armenian ministers who are pastors of American Protestant churches in this coun-

try. Most Armenians who adopt Protestantism incline to
become Congregationalists or Presbyterians, largely the former.
Then there is the Armenian Orthodox Church, which is the
national church, and a small per cent. of the Armenians are
Roman Catholics. From 75 to 90 per cent. of the whole nation
is said to belong to the Orthodox Church.

POLITICS—In American politics the Armenians are vari-
ously Democrats or Republicans. There are a few Socialists,
whose aim is chiefly the social reconstruction of Armenia.
These Socialists are not at all defeatists, and are violently anti-
German and anti-Turkish. As soon as the war began they followed the example of some prominent American Socialists, in
dissociating themselves from the so-called "international"
ideals of the Socialists. As [to the reconstruction of Armenia
and the return of the younger and more active men to the home
country, we are reminded that two conditions are indispensable
—political freedom and economic security. The Armenian
National Union, which is a coalition of several Armenian societies
in this country, was not so long ago established with this chief
object. From well-informed Armenians we learn that the wish
of the people is to be done now and forever with the "unspeakable Turk." To this end they would have Armenia for the
Armenians marked off on strict geographical lines. They
realize that it will take years for them to become successfully
autonomous, and it is reported that they would not object to
some such protectorate as we established in Cuba after the
Spanish-American War. If any country outside were to have
authority in Armenia they would prefer the United States. But
they are fixt in their determination to be nationally self-deter-
mined and believe that the old order must yield to the new.

ARMENIANS IN AMERICA
1920

A short but very interesting article
on the situation of the Armenians in
America — based on materials prepared by Rev. Joseph Kafafian Thomson — is reproduced below.

Source: <u>Outlook</u>, February 25, 1920.

JUST now hundreds of thousands of Armenians are hoping and praying that the United States will take a mandate from the League of Nations to protect and help govern Armenia. If one argues that this ought to be done, it is pertinent for him to show that Armenians have the stuff of which good citizens are made. America's interest in Armenians has naturally expressed itself mainly in sympathy for the sufferings of Armenians in their own land. We are glad, therefore, to give publicity to the following sketch of what Armenians have done in America. This comes to us from the Rev. Joseph Kafafian Thomson, a naturalized American of Armenian parentage. Mr. Thomson, who is a graduate of Drew Theological Seminary and the Yale School of Religion, is now an ordained minister preaching at several places in coal and lumber towns in West Virginia. He writes as follows:

" 'Martin ye Armeanean' was a member of the Colony at Jamestown, Virginia, in 1618. He came here as one of the servants of Governor Yeardley. While in Virginia he acquired British citizenship, which entitled him to the distinction of being the first naturalized person on the American continent.

" In 1653 Edward Diggs brought over at his own expense two Armenians who were expert cultivators of silkworms. The result of their work was so promising that in December, 1656, the Virginia Assembly passed the following resolution: 'That George the Armenian for his encouragement in the silk trade and to stay in the country, have four thousand pounds of tobacco allowed him by the assembly.'

" In 1813 American missionaries went to Turkey and established schools. Armenian students began to come to America in 1834. They received degrees from Princeton, Yale, and other universities. Der Seropian inaugurated the class-book custom at Yale. He is also credited with having discovered the green color now used on all United States currency. So it was an Armenian who put the green in our 'greenback.'

"After the massacres of 1894 the Armenian 'exiles' began to arrive in greater numbers. In the true sense of the word the Armenians are not immigrants, but, like the Pilgrims of 1620, they come to America for religious liberty. After each massacre Armenians arrive in greater numbers. The statistics of the Commissioner of Immigration disclose certain valuable data concerning the character of the Armenians. The percentage of skilled laborers and professional men is greater than in any other race coming from southern Europe or Asia. The average income of an Armenian family composed of wage-earners was found to be $730; Greek family, $632; Hebrew family, $685; north Italian, $657; south Italian, $569; Serbian, $462; Polish, $595; Russian, $494; Slovak, $582; and Syrian, $594.

"The Armenian farmers have made good in California. Armenians handle eighty per cent of the Oriental rugs that come to America. There are over one hundred Armenian clergymen; thirty-nine of these preach to American congregations. The number of Armenian doctors and dentists exceeds two hundred. Armenian lawyers now in active practice number fifteen. There are a great number of engineers, chemists, architects, and editors of Armenian and American papers.

There are eleven professors and instructors in our leading universities. Two of the most noted photographers in the United States are Armenians. There are well-known painters and sculptors who have won prizes in New York, Chicago, and San Francisco. There are Armenians on the stage and distinguished operatic singers, several of whom appear at the Metropolitan Opera House, New York. Of all the Armenians admitted in this country between 1899 and 1910, only 23.9 per cent could not read or write, while among .other nationalities the percentage of illiteracy is as follows : Greeks, 26.4 ; Hebrews, 26 ; Rumanians, 35 ; Bulgarians, 41.7 ; southern Italians, 54.8 ; Polish, 35.4 ; Portuguese, 68.2 ; Russians, 35.4 ; and Syrians, 53.3.

" The number of Armenian students in American colleges and universities in 1916 was 234. When we consider the fact that there are less than one hundred thousand Armenians in America, this is a better record than that of any other foreign people and is as good as that of the native-born American. In 1916 there were at the Yale School of Religion only three Armenians—one won the Dean's prize and another a leading scholarship. In the same year at Wesleyan University there was only one Armenian. He won more prizes in oratory and debate than any other man in that university, and he was competing with men ninety per cent of whom were native-born Americans, while he had learned not one word of English from his parents. Armenians have married American women and are raising American families. These marriages, as a rule, turn out well. Armenians become Americanized faster than any other people who come to America. They head the list in becoming naturalized citizens. Thousands of them enlisted in the late war. They make good soldiers, sailors, and marines. There are no Armenian tramps or beggars in America. This is the type and quality of people, a million of whose relatives have left their bleached bones on the sands of Asia Minor because they were determined to remain Christian.

" According to Herbert Hoover, ' the situation in the Near East is the most desperate in the world.' Here eight hundred thousand Armenians, mostly women and children, are starving. One report states that they have dug up cemeteries to chew on the bones of the dead. No language is adequate to describe their misery. There are two and only two ways to help them. First, through the Near East Relief Committee, 1 Madison Avenue, New York City ; and, second, by influencing Congress to recognize the independence of Armenia."

The Council of Ambassadors, the successor of the Supreme Council of the Paris Peace Conference, has now recognized the independence of the *de facto* Armenian Government.

PRESIDENT WOODROW WILSON SUPPORTING THE
ARMENIAN CAUSE
1920

In response to the sympathy of the American people for the Armenian cause, as
well as to the wishes expressed by the
majority of Armenian Americans and their
conationals residing in the Republic of
Armenia, President Woodrow Wilson sent
a message to the United States Congress
requesting that the Congress grant executive power to accept for the United
States a mandate for Armenia. The text
of the message, dated May 24, 1920, follows below.

Source: U.S. Statutes at Large, 66th
Congress (1919-1920), 2nd Session,
House of Representative Document No.
791.

MANDATE FOR ARMENIA.

MESSAGE

FROM THE

PRESIDENT OF THE UNITED STATES,

REQUESTING

**THAT THE CONGRESS GRANT THE EXECUTIVE POWER TO ACCEPT
FOR THE UNITED STATES A MANDATE FOR ARMENIA.**

MAY 24, 1920.—Read; referred to the Committee on Foreign Affairs, and ordered
to be printed.

GENTLEMEN OF THE CONGRESS:

On the fourteenth of May an official communication was received
at the Executive Office from the Secretary of the Senate of the United
States conveying the following preambles and resolutions:

Whereas the testimony adduced at the hearings conducted by the subcommittee of
the Senate Committee on Foreign Relations have clearly established the truth of
the reported massacres and other atrocities from which the Armenian people have
suffered; and

Whereas the people of the United States are deeply impressed by the deplorable
conditions of insecurity, starvation, and misery now prevalent in Armenia; and

Whereas the independence of the Republic of Armenia has been duly recognized by the Supreme Council of the Peace Conference and by the Government of the United States of America: Therefore be it

Resolved, That the sincere congratulations of the Senate of the United States are hereby extended to the people of Armenia on the recognition of the independence of the Republic of Armenia, without prejudice respecting the territorial boundaries involved: And be it further

Resolved, That the Senate of the United States hereby expresses the hope that stable government, proper protection of individual liberties and rights, and the full realization of nationalistic aspirations may soon be attained by the Armenian people: And be it further

Resolved, That in order to afford necessary protection for the lives and property of citizens of the United States at the port of Batum and along the line of the railroad leading to Baku, the President is hereby requested, if not incompatible with the public interest, to cause a United States warship and a force of marines to be dispatched to such port with instructions to such marines to disembark and to protect American lives and property.

I received and read this document with great interest and with genuine gratification, not only because it embodied my own convictions and feelings with regard to Armenia and its people, but also, and more particularly, because it seemed to me the voice of the American people expressing their genuine convictions and deep Christian sympathies, and intimating the line of duty which seemed to them to lie clearly before us.

I cannot but regard it as providential, and not as a mere casual coincidence that almost at the same time I received information that the conference of statesmen now sitting at San Remo for the purpose of working out the details of peace with the Central Powers which it was not feasible to work out in the conference at Paris, had formally resolved to address a definite appeal to this Government to accept the mandate for Armenia. They were at pains to add that they did this, "not from the smallest desire to evade any obligations which they might be expected to undertake, but because the responsibilities which they are already obliged to bear in connection with the disposition of the former Ottoman Empire will strain their capacities to the uttermost, and because they believe that the appearance on the scene of a power emancipated from the prepossessions of the old world will inspire a wider confidence and afford a firmer guarantee for stability in the future than would the selection of any European power."

Early in the conferences at Paris it was agreed that to those colonies and territories which as a consequence of the late war have ceased to be under the sovereignty of the States which formerly governed them and which are inhabited by peoples not yet able to stand by themselves under the strenuous conditions of the modern world there should be applied the principle that the well being and development of such peoples form a sacred trust of civilization, and that securities for the performance of this trust should be afforded.

It was recognized that certain communities formerly belonging to the Turkish Empire have reached a stage of development where their existence as independent nations can be provisionally recognized, subject to the rendering of administrative advice and assistance by a mandatory until such time as they are able to stand alone.

It is in pursuance of this principle and with a desire of affording Armenia such advice and assistance that the statesmen conferring at San Remo have formally requested this Government to assume the duties of mandatory in Armenia. I may add, for the information of the Congress, that at the same sitting it was resolved to request the President of the United States to undertake to arbitrate the difficult question of the boundary between Turkey and Armenia in the Vilayets of Erzerum, Trebizond, Van and Bitlis, and it was agreed to accept his decision thereupon, as well as any stipulation he may prescribe as to access to the sea for the independent State of Armenia. In pursuance of this action, it was resolved to embody in the Treaty with Turkey, now under final consideration, a provision that "Turkey and Armenia and the other High Contracting Parties agree to refer to the arbitration of the President of the United States of America the question of the boundary between Turkey and Armenia in the Vilayets of Erzerum, Trebizond, Van and Bitlis, and to accept his decision thereupon as well as any stipulation he may prescribe as to access to the sea for the independent State of Armenia;" pending

that decision the boundaries of Turkey and Armenia to remain as at present. I have thought it my duty to accept this difficult and delicate task.

In response to the invitation of the Council at San Remo, I urgently advise and request that the Congress grant the Executive power to accept for the United States a mandate over Armenia. I make this suggestion in the earnest belief that it will be the wish of the people of the United States that this should be done. The sympathy with Armenia has proceeded from no single portion of our people, but has come with extraordinary spontaneity and sincerity from the whole of the great body of Christian men and women in this country by whose free-will offerings Armenia has practically been saved at the most critical juncture of its existence. At their hearts this great and generous people have made the cause of Armenia their own. It is to this people and to their Government that the hopes and earnest expectations of the struggling people of Armenia turn as they now emerge from a period of indescribable suffering and peril, and I hope that the Congress will think it wise to meet this hope and expectation with the utmost liberality. I know from unmistakable evidences given by responsible representatives of many peoples struggling towards independence and peaceful life again that the Government of the United States is looked to with extraordinary trust and confidence, and I believe that it would do nothing less than arrest the hopeful processes of civilization if we were to refuse the request to become the helpful friends and advisers of such of these people as we may be authoritatively and formally requested to guide and assist.

I am conscious that I am urging upon the Congress a very critical choice, but I make the suggestion in the confidence that I am speaking in the spirit and in accordance with the wishes of the greatest of the Christian peoples. The sympathy for Armenia among our people has sprung from untainted consciences, pure Christian faith, and an earnest desire to see Christian people everywhere succored in their time of suffering, and lifted from their abject subjection and distress and enabled to stand upon their feet and take their place among the free nations of the world. Our recognition of the independence of Armenia will mean genuine liberty and assured happiness for her people, if we fearlessly undertake the duties of guidance and assistance involved in the functions of a mandatory. It is, therefore, with the most earnest hopefulness and with the feeling that I am giving advice from which the Congress will not willingly turn away that I urge the acceptance of the invitation now formally and solemnly extended to us by the Council at San Remo, into whose hands has passed the difficult task of composing the many complexities and difficulties of government in the one-time Ottoman Empire and the maintenance of order and tolerable conditions of life in those portions of that Empire which it is no longer possible in the interest of civilization to leave under the government of the Turkish authorities themselves.

WOODROW WILSON.

THE WHITE HOUSE, 24 May, 1920.

ARMENIAN STUDIES PROGRAM AT THE UNIVER-
SITY OF CALIFORNIA
1960 - 1973

The Armenian Studies Program at UCLA was
inaugurated in 1960 on a modest scale,
but in the following decade it became an
important center of higher education in
the United States, concentrated on a
broadly-based curriculum of Armenian
courses, and offering graduate degree
programs in Armenian studies. Here are
some highlights regarding the history,
activities and achievements of the Armenian Studies Program at UCLA.

Source: Report for 1960-1973, The
Armenian Studies Program at UCLA.

I. Preliminary Program

The Armenian Studies Program of UCLA was inauguarated in 1960
on a modest scale, as part of the Master Plan for the development
of Near Eastern Studies at the Los Angeles campus of the University
of California under the direction of the late Professor Gustav E.
von Grunebaum. Until 1965, the Program was staffed by the following temporary personnel: Dr. Louise Nalbandian (1960-61), Dr. A.O.
Sarkissian of the Library of Congress (Fall semester 1961-62), and
Dr. Kevork Sarafian, Emeritus (Spring semester 1962). These individuals taught several courses in Armenian language and history.
Dr. Richard Hovannisian, then a graduate student at UCLA, taught
similar courses during the years 1962-66. During the academic year
1963-64, the Very Rev. Sempad Lapajian also offered a course in
Armenian language.

Besides the offerings at UCLA in 1961-63, Mr. Hovannisian
organized University of California Extension Courses in Armenian
Cultural Heritage and Language in Fresno, California, with more
than 100 persons enrolled annually for credit. Similarly, he organized University of California Extension Courses in Armenian
Cultural Heritage at UCLA and San Fernando Valley, through the
University Extension Evening Division in 1963-64, with 15-20
students in each course.

In 1965, with the appointment of Dr. Avedis K. Sanjian (formerly of Harvard University) as associate Professor of Armenian with
tenure in the Department of Near Eastern Languages, UCLA emerged
from its modest beginning to become one of the few institutions of

higher learning in the United States concentrating on the Armenian aspect of the broader field of Caucasian, as well as Indo-European, studies. As a result of this appointment, the Department of Near Eastern Languages began to offer a broadly-based curriculum of Armenian courses encompassing instruction in Classical and Modern Armenian, both on three levels (elementary, intermediate, and advanced); Survey of Armenian Literature; Seminar in Armenian Historiography; and Special Studies in Armenian Language and Literature. These nine courses were supplemented by two others in the Department of History, namely, Armenian Intellectual History (offered by Dr. Sankian), and Armenian History (taught by Mr. Hovannisian since 1962).

II The Armenian Endowment and Establishment of the Chair for Armenian Studies

In 1962 an agreement was reached between the National Association for Armenian Studies and Research (NAASR) and the University of California whereby NAASR was authorized to use the name of the University in a fund-raising campaign, one purpose of which was to be tee establishing of an Endowed Chair for Armenian Studies at UCLA. Specifically, the University of California Board of Regents Agreed:

"That the NAASR be authorized to use the name of the University in a fund-raising campaign for the purpose of establishing a $1,000,000 Permanent Fund for the Advancement of Armenian Studies, $200,000 of which will be utilized to establish an Endowed Chair for Armenian Studies at the University of California, Los Angeles, it being understood: (a) that campaign material will receive prior approval in accordance with the University policy; (b) that $150,000 of the $200,000 will be provided within five years and the balance within three years thereafter; and (c) that the Los Angeles campus will establish and fund the Chair with a regularly budgeted tenure faculty position at the time the initial amount is received, thereafter reducing University support as the endowment income grows."

In the spring of 1969 as a result of a six-year campaign, $150,000 of the $200,000 endowment fund had been provided. Expecting a generous contribution of $25,000 by Mr. Stephen P. Mugar of Belmont, Mass., the preponderance of the funds was contributed by members of the Armenian community throughout California, particularly in Souther California.

As a result of this achievement, on May 26, 1969, Chancellor Charles E. Young announced the establishment in perpetuity of the Chair for Armenian Studies in UCLA's Department of Near Eastern Languages, with Professor Avedis K. Sankian as its first occupant. The Chancellor also announced the creation of a Program in Armenian Studies under the direction Professor Sanjian within the Near Eastern Center. To advise Dr. Sanjian in the administration of the program, Chancellor Yound appointed a steering committee consisting of the late Dr. Gustav von Grunebaum, Director of the Near Eastern Center, chairman; Dr. Malcolm H. Kerr, then chairman of the Department of Political Science; Dr. Andreas Tietze, then chairman of the Department of Near Eastern Languages; and Professor Sanjian. (Currently, the steering committee is composed of Dr. Speros Vryonis, Director of the Near Eastern Center, and Professor Kerr, Hovannisian, and Sanjian.) The Chancellor also announced that a regular teaching position in the field of Armenian history will be established in the Department of History. In the fall of 1969, Dr. Richard Hovannisian (who since 1966 ahad been teaching full-time at Mount St. Mary's College in Los Angeles, and teaching Armenian history part-time at UCLA) was appointed to this positon as an Associate Professor.

As a reslut of these measures, Armenian Studies at UCLA were firmly anchored in two regular academic departments, that is, in the Department of Near Eastern Languages where the armenian language and literature courses are offered, and in the Department of History where the courses in Armenian history are taught. This arrangement accommodates students concentrating in the linguistic, literary, philological, and historical fields.

Beginning in 1966, the instructional staff has also included annually a graduate student as Teaching Assistant in the Department of Near Eastern Languages, whose responsibility has been to teach the courses in elementary and intermediate Modern Armenian language. This position has been held, successively, by the following: Mrs. Alice Keshishian, Mr. Raffi Setian, Mr. Yeghia Babikian, and currently by Mr. Hagop Hagopian. Moveover, from 1965 to 1967 the Near Eastern Center appointed Dr. George Egan as post-doctoral research fellow in Armenain Studies.

III Change in the Terms of the Endowment

When the campaign was initiated in 1963 to raise funds for the establishment of an Endowed Chair for Armenian Studies at UCLA, it was contemplated that—in the fashion of privately-supported institutions—the income from the endowment would be used each year for the payment of the salary of the professor who was honored to occupy the chair. If additonal income were available from the fund a second professor of Armenian Studies would be appointed and his salary paid from such income. Lastly, if any funds were still available, they would be used to support the research and programs of an Armenian Studies Program.

In 1970 the UCLA administrative authorities felt that a change in the above-stated priorities should be made in view of the following considerations. UCLA had established the Armenian Chair, had appointed two tenured professors, and had acquired a large private library of Armenian manuscripts, books, and archival materials—all without having access to income from the Armenian endowment fund. The two regular, tenured faculty positions have been

funded by the state budget. As a matter of fact, the annual income
from the endowment would not be sufficient to pay the salary of
either of the two Armenian scholars. The UCLA contribution to the
Armenian Studies Program has been substantial. If the salaries of
the two professors and other expenses connected with Armenian Studies
now being borne entirely by UCLA, were paid out of the income from
an endowment, that endowment would have to approximate $1,000,000.

In view of the above, a change in the terms of the endowment
was deemed necessary. At the suggestion of the UCLA administrative
authorities, and with the concurrence of the NAASR Board of Direc-
tors as well as a large majority of the donors, the fund was re-
named the "UCLA Armenain Studies Endowment Fund," and the income
from this fund was to be used to support, broaden and enrich the
Armenian Studies Program at UCLA rather than to pay the salary of
the occupant of the chair. This arrangment would provide funds
to make further library acquisitions; to incite visiiing professors and lecturers; to hold colloquia and seminars; to travel to
conferences concerned with Armenian Studies--in short, to extend
the functions of the program beyond what two faculty members can
do as teachers and individual researchers.

The perpetuity of the Chair for Armenian Studies is assured
by the fact that, if necessary, the income from the endowment
will always be first applied to the salary of the holder of the
Chair. The income of the fund will be used to support the Chair,
in the manner described above, only if the salary is available--
as at present--from other sources. Thus, the original purpose--
the establishment of a Chair for Armenian Studies in perpetuity--
is guaranteed, and UCLA will have the flexiblity in the use of
the funds necessary to permit the Armenian Studies Program to
flourish.

IV Graduate Degree Programs in Armenian Studies

In the fall of 1969, the UCLA Graduate Division approved
Armenian as an area of specializaiion for the M.A. and Ph.D. de-
grees in Near Eastern Languages. Simultaneously, the Graduate
Division also approved Armenian History as an area of specializa-
tion for the M.A. and Ph.D. degrees in the Department of History.
Both actions were based on the fact that Professors Sanjian and
Hovannisian had augmented the teaching cirricula in their respec-
tive departments with a considerable number of graduate courses.

VIII Armenian Library Collections

The instructional and research programs at UCLA utilize what
we believe is the largest fund of Armenian research in the United
States. This collection has had a steady growth since 1961 and
now comprises some 10,000 volumes. The following is a summary
account of the growth as well as the scope of the Armenian holdings.

In 1961, the UCLA Research Library received as a bequest the

private library of the late Dr. K.M. Khantamour, comprising a
collection of some 1000 out-of-print books mainly in the fields
of Armenian history, literature, and folklore. In 1966-67,
Professors Sanjian and Hovannisian acquired some 500 volumes as
gifts from institutions in Erevan, Armenia, following individual
visits there. In 1967, the Library also secured 87 reels of
microfilmed Armenian periodicals and newspapers through the services of Dr. Louise Nalbandian, formerly instructor in Armenian
language and history at UCLA.

In 1968, UCLA purchased an outstanding and perhaps the
world's largest private library of printed books, manuscripts,
and archival materials belonging to the late Dr. Caro O. Minasian
of Isfahan, Iran. This acquisition was made possible due to the
concerted efforts of a number of UCLA administrative officials
and faculty staff, but especially to Professor Sanjian who initiated and finalized the negotiations with the owner and secured
its shipment to UCLA. With the exception of a most generous
contribution of $25,000 from Mr. Alex Manoogian of Detroit,
Michigan, UCLA accomplished the purchase of this unique library
with its own resources and at a cost of many times that amount.

Accumulated during the lifetime of a single individual,
this private library consists of some 10,000 printed books,
manuscripts, and archival documents in Armenian, as well as
various Near Eastern and European languages. The Armenian, portion comprises approximately 4000 volumes and includes some 150
manuscripts; about 1000 early printed and rare books in the
fields of history, language, and literature; early runs of several valuable journals that are no longer published; a large
group of rare Indian-Armenian books and periodicals; and a large
number of 19th and 20th century materials on a variety of subjects.

The Armenian manuscripts in this collection put UCLA in
the front rank of such holdings in the United States. (This is
underscored by the fact that, until UCLA's acquisitions, the
Hartford Seminary in Connecticut had the largest collection,
with only 22 Armenian manuscripts.) Professor Sanjian has already prepared a brief hand-list of the manuscripts and is
planning to prepare a detailed descriptive catalogue in the
near future. Included in this collection is a copy of the Four
Gospels, containing exquisite illuminations executed at the
famous monastery of Gladzor in the first half of the 14th century by T'oros Taronatsi, one of the three outstanding medieval
Armenian miniaturists.

The Minasian Collection also contains thousands of archival materials and documents, including ecclesiastical
encyclicals and governmental edicts, private papers of Armenian
clergymen and mercantile families in Iran and India, numerous
historical photographs of Armenian interest, and so forth.

As a result of the steady acquisition of Armenian materials by purchase (including purchase of small libraries), as well as gifts and exchange, the UCLA Research Library now has amassed a total of some 10,000 volumes, including approximately 150 periodical titles, 90 reels of microfilm, and 40 sets of periodicals and newspapers, many of which are no longer published. Moreover, the Library currently receives 47 Armenian periodicals and newspapers as gifts or on exchange.

Since 1967, Miss A. Gia Aivazian has been responsible for the acquisition and cataloguing of the Armenian materials in the UCLA Research Library. Miss Aivazian was instrumental in devising new and detailed schemes for the classification, numbering, and subject headings for Armenian materials, which were adopted by the Library of Congress in 1971. This is considered a major contribution to the system of bibliographical control for Armenian materials in the United States. Miss Aivazian is planning to prepare a bibliography of the Library's holdings of early Armenian printed books as well as rare books numbering some 1000 volumes and now deposited in the Library's Department of Special Collections. These rare books include the significant number of Indian-Armenian imprints, which constitute perhaps one of the largest such holdings in the world. A separate bibliography of these materials is also contemplated.

It is expected that by 1975 the major portion of the Armenian collections at UCLA will have been catalogued. It should be noted that the Armenian Assembly has approved and has funded a project involving the preparation of a "Union Catalogue of Armenian Materials in the United States Libraries." This project will be carried out at UCLA under the direction of Miss Aivazian and the general supervision of Professor Sanjian. The UCLA holdings will constitute the basic part of the proposed "Catalogue." Other major holdings represented will be those in the Library of Congress, the New York Public Library, the libraries at Harvard, Columbia, the University of California at Berkeley, as well as several other institutional libraries in the United States.

The Armenian collection is, of course, becoming known outside of the UCLA community, as evidenced by the increasing number of reference queries and interlibrary borrowing. It is expected that the latter form of use will be considerable increased when the aforementioned "Union Catalogue" and the smaller bibliographies are completed and published.

IX. Armenian Scholarship Funds

1. In september 1971, Mr. Armen G. Avedisian, Chairman of the Board of Avedisian Industries, Inc., and his sister, Mrs. Alice Ann Avedisian McAlister, both of Chicago, Illinois, contributed the sum of $10,000 to set up "The Karekin Der

Avedisian Memorial Endowment Scholarship Fund" in memory of
their father. According to the terms of the Endowment, the
UCLA Foundation is to invest the principal and use the income
for scholarship, thus insuring the perpetuity of the scholarship fund. The scholarship is to be given to undergraduates,
graduates, or post-doctoral students whose major is in Armenian
Studies, with no restrictions as to sex or citizenship. The
scholarship may be given either to students with financial need
or those with outstanding academic ability. The awardee should
be selected by the occupant of the Chair of Armenian Studies.

   2. In February 1973, Mrs. Siroon Hovannisian of Fresno,
California, and the families of her four sons (including Professor Richard Hovannisian of UCLA) established the "Kasper
Hovannisian Memorial Scholarship for Armenian Studies" at UCLA,
in memory of her husband and their father. The endowment of
$15,000 to be administered through the UCLA Foundation, will
provide an annual scholarship for a student enrolled in a program
leading to an advanced degree in Armenian history, language, or
literature or to a student in any discipline whose dissertation
topic pertains to the Armenian people. The endowment is intended to support the Armenian program at UCLA and to serve as
a lasting tribute to the late Kasper Hovannisian.

   3. Mr. Alex Manoogian, President of the Armenian General
Benevolent Union and well-known philanthropist, has generously
contributed an annual sum of $3,000 to the University. This
fund has been put at the disposal of Professor Sanjian and it
has been used for the needs of the Armenian program, particularly
as grants-in-aid to needy and scholastically deserving students
concentrating in the field of Armenian Studies.

X. Exhibitions

   1. The UCLA Museum of Ethnic Arts and the Armenian Studies
Program jointly sponsored an exhibition entitled: "Armenia: A
Millennium of Culture, Xth to XXth Centuries," at the UCLA Ethnic
Art Galleries. The display was originally scheduled form June 9
through 30, 1970; the success of the exhibition necessitated its
extension through July 31, 1970. The exhibition was officially
opened on Sunday, June 7, 1970, with a garden reception given by
Chancellor and Mrs. Charles E. Young for University officials
and Armenian community patrons of the exhibition.

   The display, organized by Mr. J. D. Frierman, then acting
chief curator of the Museum, and Professor Sanjian, represented
one of the most extensive and important displays of Armenian art
and folk culture ever assembled in the United States. The show
spanned Armenian culture from the 10th to 20th centuries and included over 50 extremely rare and beautiful medieval illuminated
manuscripts and an exceptionally fine collection of 27 inscribed

and dated Armenian rugs. Ecclesiastical works included rare
18th and 19th century silver and silver-gilt objects, from
chalices to episcopal crowns, a large group of Kutahya ceramics,
and four unusually large and superbly executed altar curtains
--two of silkbrocade woven in Bursa and two printed and painted
curtains from New Julfa, Iran. Other works included a large
selection of textiles ranging from medieval ecclesiastical vest-
ments to secular garments of the 18th century, folk costumes,
and domestic fabrics, plus many copper, brass and bronze vessels,
elaborately engraved with Armenian inscriptions.

Mr. Harry Kurdian of Witchita, Kansas, and Mr. Haroutioune
Hazarian of New York City, whose collections are considered among
the finest and largest private holdings of Armenian art in the
world, were principal lenders to the exhibition. Other works
were obtained through the generosity of private collectors
throughout California, and from the UCLA Library Special Collections. Private collectors who contributed to the exhibition
included: Mr. A. H. Dickranian, G. A. Gertmenian and Sons,
J.H. Minassian and Co., Mr. Albert Nalbandian, Dr. Louise
Nalbandian, Dr. Katherine Otto-Dorn, and Pashgian Bros.

Designed by Professor Jack Carter of UCLA, the exhibition
installation also featured taped Armenian music and slide pro-
jections including a wide range of slides on Armenian church
architecture of the Middle Ages.

Chancellor Young wrote in the Foreword of the exhibition's
brochure: "The exhibition 'A Millennium of Armenian Culture,'
the first of its kind in this country, will stand out as a high
point of the Armenian program in this university. Its beauty
should be taken as a tribute to Armenian culture and as a symbol
of what this university expects to do in the Armenian field.
No better occasion could be thought of to reaffirm with enthu-
siasm UCLA's long-standing commitment to Armenian Studies."
Dr. G. E. von Grunebaum, Director of the UCLA Near Eastern
Center, also wrote: ". . . We consider it an obligation of
effective scholarship as much as an obligation of service to
the public to exhibit, for all to see, the greatness of a
civilization and the people who created and carried it on, and
to do so in the most convincing, because the most objective, way.
It is through the eye that character and style, aspiration and
accomplishment of a civilization can most strikingly and most
persuasively be conveyed."

The entire cost of the exhibition, amounting to over
$13,000, was underwritten by UCLA from the income of the Ar-
menian Endowment Fund. Unfortunately, the prohibitive cost
prevented the anticipated publication of an illustrated catalogue
describing all the objects displayed.

2. The Department of Near Eastern Languages, the Near
Eastern Center, and the Museum of Ethnic Arts, jointly sponsored an exhiibtion "The Near East in UCLA Collections," held
at UCLA in May-June 1969. This included a selection of handsome manuscript volumes in Persian, Arabic, and Armenian from
the UCLA Research Library's Department of Special Collections.

According to art critic Henry Seldis of the Los Angeles
Times (June 2, 1969 issue): "Among the manuscripts shown, the
rarest and most ornate are early 14th-century and late 15th-
century Armenian folios that offer outstanding examples of
medieval Armenian miniature painting at its best . . ." The
reference is to two Armenian Gospel manuscripts on vellum from the
the UCLA collection: the first executed at the famous medieval
Armenian monastery of Gladzor for an Armenian princely family
which ruled in the province of Siwnik'. Its illuminations were
executed by T'oros Taronatsi, one of the three most outstanding
Armenian miniaturists. The second Gospel was executed in 1481
by an unknown scribe and artist. It is probably the smallest
vellum Gospel in Armenian in existence today. Also included in
the exhibit were two copies of the first printing of the Armenian Bible by Voskan Yerevantsi at Amsterdam, Holland, in 1666.
The first copy is on bluish paper, and the second on yellowish
paper.

WILLIAM SAROYAN, PROMINENT ARMENIAN AMERICAN WRITER
1969

William Saroyan, a prominent contemporary literary figure, especially known for his short stories and plays, started his literary career in the middle of the 1930's. The following excerpts reveal interesting facets of Saroyan's life and writings.

Source: Contemporary Authors. Detroit, Michigan: Gale Research Company, 1969, vol. 5-8, First Revision. Permission to reprint by Gale Research Company.

SAROYAN, William   1908-
(Sirak Goryan)

PERSONAL: Born August 31, 1908, in Fresno, Calif.; son of Armenak (a Presbyterian preacher and a writer) and Takoohi (Saroyan) Saroyan; married Carol Marcus, February, 1943 (divorced, November, 1949; remarried Carol Marcus, 1951 (again divorced, 1952); children: Aram (a writer), Lucy. *Education:* Left high school at fifteen. *Home:* 114 rue la Boetie, Paris 8e, France.

CAREER: Began selling newspapers at the age of eight for the *Fresno Evening Herald;* while still in school he worked at various jobs, including that of telegraph messenger boy; after leaving school he worked in his uncle's law office, then held numerous odd jobs, including that of grocery clerk, vineyard worker, postal employee, and office manager of San Francisco Postal Telegraph Co. Co-founder of Conference Press, 1936. Organized and directed The Saroyan Theatre, August, 1942 (closed after one week). Writer in residence, Purdue University, 1961. *Military service:* U.S. Army, 1942-45. *Awards, honors:* Drama Critics Circle Award, 1940, for "The Time of Your Life"; Pulitzer Prize, 1940, for "The Time of Your Life" (Saroyan rejected the prize, saying he was opposed to the patronizing of art by the wealthy; "The Time of Your Life" was the first play to ever win both awards); California Literature Gold Medal, 1952, for *Tracy's Tiger.*

WRITINGS: The Daring Young Man on the Flying Trapeze, and Other Stories, Random, 1934, 3rd edition, Modern Library, 1941; *A Christmas Psalm,* Gelber, Lilienthal, 1935; *Inhale and Exhale* (stories), Random, 1936; *Those Who Write Them and Those Who Collect Them,* Black Archer Press, 1936; *Three Times Three* (stories), Conference Press, 1936; *Little Children* (stories), Harcourt, 1937; *A Gay and Melancholy Flux* (compiled

from *Inhale and Exhale* and *Three Times Three,* Faber, 1937; *Love, Here is My Hat, and Other Short Romances,* Modern Age Books, 1938; *The Trouble with Tigers* (stories), Harcourt, 1938; *A Native American,* George Fields, 1938; *Peace, It's Wonderful* (stories), Modern Age Books, 1939; *3 Fragments and a Story,* Little Man, 1939; *The Hungerers: A Short Play,* S. French, 1939; *My Heart's in the Highlands* (play; produced at Guild Theatre, New York, April 13, 1939; first published in *One-Act Play Magazine,* December, 1937), Harcourt, 1939; *The Time of Your Life* (play; produced at Booth Theatre, New York, October 25, 1939), Harcourt, 1939; *Christmas, 1939,* Quercus Press, 1939.

"A Theme in the Life of the Great American Goof" (ballet-play; produced at Center Theatre, New York, January, 1940), published in *Razzle-Dazzle,* below; *Subway Circus* (play), S. French, 1940; *The Ping-Pong Game* (play), S. French, 1940; *Three Plays,* Harcourt, 1940; *A Special Announcement,* House of Books, 1940; *My Name is Aram* (stories; Book-of-the-Month Club selection), Harcourt, 1940, 4th edition, Harbrace Modern Classics, 1950; *The Beautiful People* (play; produced and directed by the author at Lyceum Theatre, New York, April 21, 1940), Harcourt, 1941; *Saroyan's Fables,* Harcourt, 1941; *Love's Old Sweet Song* (play; produced at Plymouth Theatre, New York, May 2, 1940), S. French, 1941; *Harlem as Seen by Hirschfield,* Hyperion Press, 1941, *Hilltop Russians in San Francisco,* James Ladd Delkin, 1941; *Jim Dandy: A Play,* [Cleveland], 1941, reprinted as *Jim Dandy: Fat Man in a Famine,* Harcourt, 1947; "Across the Board on Tomorrow Morning," first produced at Pasadena (Calif.) Playhouse, February, 1941, produced at Theatre Showcase, March, 1942, another production produced and directed by the author at Belasco Theatre, New York, on the same bill with "Talking to You," also produced and directed by the

author, August, 1942; *Hello Out There* (play; first produced at Lobeto Theatre, Santa Barbara, September,
1941, produced at Belasco Theatre, September, 1942), S.
French, 1949; *Razzle-Dazzle* (short plays), Harcourt,
1942; *48 Saroyan Stories*, Avon, 1942; *The Human
Comedy* (novel adapted from his film scenario), Har-
court, 1943, 4th edition. World Publishing, 1945; *Thirty-
One Selected Stories*, Avon, 1943; *Fragment*, Albert M.
Bender, 1943; *Get Away Old Man* (play; produced at
Cort Theatre, New York, November, 1943), Harcourt,
1944; *Some Day I'll Be a Millionaire Myself*, Avon, 1944;
Dear Baby (stories), Harcourt, 1944; *The Adventures of
Wesley Jackson* (novel), Harcourt, 1946; *The Saroyan
Special*, Harcourt, 1948; *The Fiscal Hoboes*, Press of
Valenti Angelo, 1949; *Don't Go Away Mad, and Two
Other Plays*, Harcourt, 1949; *A Decent Birth, A Happy
Funeral* (play), S. French, 1949; *Sam Ego's House* (play),
S. French, 1949.

The Assyrian, and Other Stories, Harcourt, 1950; *The
Twin Adventures* (contains *The Adventures of Wesley
Jackson* and a diary Saroyan kept while writing the
novel), Harcourt, 1950; *Rock Wagram* (novel), Doubleday, 1951; *Tracy's Tiger* (fantasy), Doubleday, 1951;
The Bicycle Rider in Beverly Hills (autobiography),
Scribner, 1952; *The Laughing Matter* (novel), Doubleday,
1953; *Mama I Love You* (novel), Atlantic-Little, Brown,
1956; *The Whole Voyald* (stories), Atlantic-Little, Brown,
1956; *The Bouncing Ball* (an erroneous citation; given in
some sources as a book published in 1957, but actually an
early title for material published as *Mama I Love You*);
Papa You're Crazy (novel), Atlantic-Little, Brown, 1957;
Pebbles on the Beach (sometimes cited as a 1957 book of
essays; no such book was published, however; *The Cave
Dwellers* (play; produced in New York, October 19,
1957), Putnam, 1958; *The William Saroyan Reader*,
Braziller, 1958; *The Slaughter of the Innocents* (play),
S. French, 1958; *Once Around the Block* (play), S. French,
1959.

"The Paris Comedy; or, The Secret of Lily" (play),
produced in Vienna, 1960, published as *The Paris Comedy; or, The Dogs, Chris Sick, and 21 Other Plays*,
Phaedra, 1969; *Sam, the Highest Jumper of Them
All, or, The London Comedy* (play; produced in
London under Saroyan's direction, 1960), Faber, 1961;
(with Henry Cecil) "Settled Out of Court" (play), produced in London, 1960; "High Time Along the Wabash"
(play), produced at Purdue University, 1961; *Here Comes,
There Goes, You Know Who* (autobiography), Trident,
1962; *Boys and Girls Together* (novel), Harcourt, 1963;
Me (juvenile), Crowell-Collier, 1963; *Not Dying* (auto-
biography), Harcourt, 1963; *One Day in the Afternoon
of the World* (novel), Harcourt, 1964; *After Thirty Years:
The Daring Young Man on the Flying Trapeze*, Harcourt,
1964; *Best Stories of William Saroyan*, Faber, 1964; *Short
Drive, Sweet Chariot* (reminiscences), Phaedra, 1966;
(author of introduction) *The Arabian Nights*, Platt, 1966;
*Look at Us; Let's See; Here We Are; Look Hard, Speak
Soft; I See, You See, We All See; Stop, Look, Listen;
Beholder's Eye; Don't Look Now But Isn't That You?
(us? U.S.?)*, Cowles, 1967; *I Used to Believe I had For-
ever, Now I'm Not So Sure*, Cowles, 1968; (author of
foreword) Barbara Holden and Mary Jane Woebcke,
A Child's Guide to San Francisco, Diablo Press, 1968;
Horsey Gorsey and the Frog, R. Hale, 1968; *Letters from
74 Rue Taitbout, or Don't Go, But If You Must, Say
Hello to Everybody*, World, 1968; *Man With the Heart in
the Highlands, and Other Stories*, Dell, 1968.

Contributor to *Overland Monthly, Hairenik* (Armenian-
American Magazine), *Story, Saturday Evening Post, Atlantic, Look, McCall's, Seventeen, Saturday Review*, and
other publications.

Wrote lyrics and music for several songs for his play,
Love's Old Sweet Song; other musical compositions
include "An Italian Opera in English," "Notes for a
Musical Review," and "Bad Men in the West" (a
ballet scenario), all published in *Razzle-Dazzle;* with Ross
Bagdasarian, wrote popular song, "Come On-a My
House," 1951. Wrote and directed a short film of
his own, "The Good Job," produced by Loew, 1942,
based on his story "A Number of the Poor"; wrote a
scenario for "The Human Comedy" for M-G-M, filmed
in 1943; *The Time of Your Life* was filmed by United
Artists, 1948. A television adaptation of *The Time of
Your Life* was produced on "Playhouse 90," October,
1958; "Ah Sweet Mystery of Mrs. Murphy" was produced
by NBC-TV, 1959; "The Unstoppable Gray Fox" was
produced by CBS-TV, 1962.

SIDELIGHTS: The untutored, personal, homely, and
human talent of Saroyan is the epitome of *gemuetlich*
sentiment in America. He arrived on the literary scene at
a time of great cynicism, yet he affirmed a kind of
nineteenth-century faith. Almost immediately he became
one of the most-discussed writers of the time, and, as
Howard R. Floan points out, "the passing years have
indicated [his] power to hold readers in large and faithful
numbers. In their closeness to folk traditions his characters reflect aspects of our national life that are too little
represented in our literature. . . . Not only has he 'charmed'
a public into existence, as Elizabeth Bowen has aptly
observed, but he has provided it with a correlative for
some of its most representative emotions." Critics called
him the most significant talent to appear in San Francisco
since Frank Norris and Jack London. He was popular,
says Floan, because he combined "the esthete's respon-
siveness to life with the stoic's resignation to the death
which he chose in preference to a mindless pursuit of
survival in an insensitive, industrialized world."

His Romantic themes have included man's innate goodness, the difficulties of immigrants asserting the virtues of
the old world, the immigrants' spiritual uprootedness,
men's dreams as they are changed by the passage of time,
and personal isolation as the ultimate tragedy. Death, for
him, is as natural as life; in fact, its closeness should lead
to an intensified view of the preciousness of life. His
outlook has been called that of a facile optimist. Floan
explains this tendency toward nostalgia and optimism
thus: "Insofar as the problems of modern man relate most
characteristically to urban, industrial situations, Saroyan
was of course turning away from subjects and themes that
seemed most central to his age. But any basic conflict
between man and his environment would have been
unlikely in Saroyan's writing because of his assumption of
the inviolability of the individual. . . . Granting Saroyan's
optimistic view of human nature, it was fortunate indeed
that he followed where his inclinations led—to the rural
and small-town environment, a setting always more con-
genial to Romanticism." There is about him something of
a Wordsworthian return to the natural man, except that
Saroyan's natural men are gas station attendants or soda
fountain boys. When *Inhale and Exhale* was published, the
Saturday Review of Literature compared its author to
Lord Byron, claiming that Saroyan displayed the same
"triumphant self-assertion." And Joseph Wood Krutch
noted: "Few men ever displayed a completer or more
clearly defined set of the stigmata of Romanticism. [Sa-
royan] accepts the universe, believes in the goodness of
the human heart, and holds that God is love. He distrusts
the respectable, rejoices in the variety of the world,
believes in the unique individual, and assumes as self-
evident that Beauty is Truth. Above all, he is convinced
that the secret of success in both life and art is to let
oneself go—as completely and as unthinkably as possible."
More recently, however, he has grappled with darker
themes in such works as *Hello Out There* and *The Cave*

Dwellers. He is even coming to believe that a man may be his own worst enemy.

He has been charged both with carelessness and sentimentality. He does not revise his work, and he has said: "I do not know a great deal about what the words come to, but the presence says, Now don't get funny; just sit down and say something; it'll be all right. Say it wrong; it'll be all right anyway. Half the time I *do* say it wrong, but somehow or other, just as the presence says, it's right anyhow. I am always pleased about this. My God, it's wrong, but it's all right. It's really all right. How did it happen? Well that's how it is. It's the presence, doing everything for me." Edmund Wilson dismisses such a statement because, he says, Saroyan is "such an engaging fellow." He adds, however, that "Saroyan is entirely in error in supposing that when he 'says it wrong,' everything is really all right. What is right in such a case is merely [an] instinctive sense of form which usually saves him—and even when he is clowning—from making a fool of himself. What *is* wrong, and what his charm cannot conceal, is the use to which he is putting his gifts." One of the strongest of these gifts, according to Wilson, is Saroyan's creation of atmosphere: "Saroyan takes you to the bar, and he creates for you there a world which is the way the world would be if it conformed to the feeling instilled by drinks. In a word, he achieves the feat of making and keeping us boozy without the use of alcohol and purely by the action of art." As for his sentimentality, Saroyan once explained that it is a very sentimental thing to be a human being. Wallace Stegner correctly asserts, however, that Saroyan's sentimental convictions "make him difficult to argue with. One can only disagree."

Because he has always been defiantly unliterary it is difficult to trace his literary influences. He bears some similarity to Sherwood Anderson, as Floan notes, in his indifference to plot, his overplaying of sincerity and spontaneity, his homely philosophy, his preference for outcasts, his contempt for formal education, and his distrust of creeds combined with a nearly mystical reverence for life. At times he sounds like Walt Whitman singing a "song of myself." His early work seemed to imitate Hemingway's in its clipped dialogue and sparse descriptions. Yet Saroyan has acknowledged only the influence of Shaw, and has hoped to have a similar effect on the public. His own estimation of himself runs thus: "I am so innately great that by comparison others who believe they are great or act as if they are great seem to me to be only pathetic, although occasionally charming."

His stories (which he sometimes wrote at the rate of one per day) have always received kinder attention than have his plays or novels. According to Elizabeth Bowen, "probably since O. Henry nobody has done more than William Saroyan to endear and stabilize the short story." Between 1934 and 1940 he wrote more than 500 stories, and, says Floan, "he learned to get into his story immediately; to fit character, setting, and mood to the action; to express with colloquial vigor what his people were capable of saying, and to imply much about what they were able to feel. His style grew lean, partly because of the influence of Hemingway and partly because of his own reaction to the criticism that he tended to talk too much. In establishing setting, he began to dispense with description altogether and to rely on simple statement. . . . Ignoring appearances and backgrounds of his characters, he began to do little more than assign names to his people and to start them talking. Because of his mastery of colloquial speech, these sketches often appeared vital and significant when they were at times no more than incomplete exercises in dramatic composition. But, at their best, they achieved moments of genuine recognition; and at such times the economy of drama became an important virtue of his story form." It should also be noted that many of his stories are based on himself and his family.

He claims, for example, that nothing in *My Name is Aram* is entirely fiction. All humanity, he believes, is contained in the "proud and angry Saroyans." Floan notes that "paradoxically, Saroyan has not been successful in straight autobiography."

His plays are fantastical, surrealistic, employing incidents rather than strong plots. Floan believes that it is a sense of pageantry which holds most of his plays together. This form "was such a fundamental departure from the main conventions of the modern drama—from the theater of ideas that has come down to us from Ibsen and Shaw—that, when Saroyan's two most remarkable plays appeared, *My Heart's in the Highlands* and *The Time of Your Life*, critics had difficulty classifying them." One critic, Jean Gould, believed that Saroyan "might well be called the Robin Goodfellow among modern American playwrights. Although the locale of his plays is far removed from the woodland scene, his Puckish humor and abundant good nature in the face of economic depression and the impending doom of war provide the atmosphere of a summer idyll in a San Francisco honky-tonk setting." And Wolcott Gibbs noted: "Whatever doubts you may have about Mr. Saroyan's status as a formal dramatist, you can't, I think, deny him one of the rightest and most fantastic imaginations in the theatre." Despite this rich imagination Saroyan's plays were not especially successful, perhaps because, as Floan suggests, Saroyan in the end always turned away from conflict. *The Time of Your Life* was his only play to achieve an extended Broadway run. David Kherdian relates how, when Saroyan realized his plays were being tampered with, he began to cast, direct, and produce his own plays on the royalties from *The Time of Your Life* and *My Name is Aram*.

Saroyan turned to writing novels in the early forties, and found scant critical favor. One reviewer objected to the "earnest-sounding mindlessness" of *Rock Wagram*, but Floan points out that the critics always seemed to miss the Eastern, mystical vagueness that was perhaps more apparent in his novels. "Everything I write," Saroyan once said, "everything I have ever written, is allegorical. This came to pass inevitably. One does not choose to write allegorically any more than one chooses to grow black hair on his head. The stories of Armenia, Kurdistan, Georgia, Persia, Syria, Arabia, Turkey and Israel are all allegorical, and apart from the fact that I heard these stories as a child told to me by both grandmothers, by great-aunts and great-uncles, and by friends of the family, I myself, am a product of Asia Minor, hence the allegorical and the real are closely related in my mind." In his later work, according to Floan, Saroyan "was in a better position to see why he had instinctively avoided ugliness and violence in his writing and had left himself open to charges of softness. It was not just sentimentality or a matter of temperament; allegory has no obligation to portray life as it is but only to select that which illustrates its themes." Floan believes, however, that Saroyan will "probably never achieve an order of success in the novel equal to that of his short fiction and his fantasies for the stage. In style, he lacks the necessary suppleness and range, and in temperament he is without the circumspective habits of mind and interest in character for its own sake that are the novelist's principal stock in trade."

Saroyan has been writing since the age of thirteen, prolifically much of the time, and he still has many pieces which remain unpublished. His purpose, he now says, is to earn as much money as possible. Because of such a candid admission, and because he has often treated serious themes casually, he has not always received the recognition which much of his work warrants. Some still consider him to be a talented amateur without realizing that, though he respects proficient and "literary" writing, he sometimes regards it as having been composed "by a fine piece of machinery instead of by a human being." As Floan, notes,

Saroyan wanted to give his readers "not art but life itself." He tended, at least in his early stories, to be somewhat solipsistic: "Either I myself was the beginning and end of the matter, or there was no matter at all," he once said. Yet, writes Floan, "by adapting his own personality to a slightly fictionalized circumstance, Saroyan imparted warmth and vitality to his protagonist, visualized his setting effectively, and conveyed through a believable conflict the tragi-comic aspect of a rather eccentric artist out of tune with his times."

BIOGRAPHICAL/CRITICAL SOURCES: Saturday Review of Literature, February 22, 1936; Edmund Wilson, The Boys in the Back Room, Colt Press, 1941; New Republic, March 9, 1953; Saturday Evening Post, August 16, 1958; Theatre Arts, December, 1958; Newsweek, March 2, 1959, September 10, 1962; Time, March 28, 1960, January 26, 1962; New York Times, January 7, 1962; New York Times Book Review, February 25, 1962; Booklover's Answer, September-October, 1963 (from which most of the above bibliography, by David Kherdian, and certain other information is taken by permission); David Kherdian, A Bibliography of William Saroyan, 1934-1964, J. Howell, 1965; Allan Lewis, American Plays and Playwrights of the Contemporary Theatre, Crown, 1965; Jean Gould, Modern American Playwrights, Dodd, 1966; Howard R. Floan, William Saroyan, Twayne, 1966.*†

ARMENIAN HERITAGE WEEK IN FRESNO,
CALIFORNIA
1975

Hon. B. F. Sisk brought to the attention of the United States the proclamation issued by Mayor Ted C. Wills
of Fresno, California, officially
designating the week of April 20,
1975, as "Armenian Heritage Week."
The following is the text of Sisk's
remarks and of the proclamation.

Source: U.S. Congressional Record,
94th Congress, (1974-1975) first
session.

FRESNO, CALIF., RESOLUTION ON
AMERICAN GENOCIDE

HON. B. F. SISK
OF CALIFORNIA
IN THE HOUSE OF REPRESENTATIVES
Tuesday, April 15, 1975

Mr. SISK. Mr. Speaker, passage last week of House Joint Resolution 148 marked the first official step toward designating April 24, 1975, as a "National Day of Remembrance of Man's Inhumanity to Man." As many of my colleagues know, this designation is prompted by the recollection of the 1915 genocide which the Armenian people endured at the hands of the Turkish nation. If an observance of this nature is to be a truly meaningful testament to the occurrence of this past atrocity and an instructive lesson in hopefully preventing future ones, the words must be accompanied by action.

I am proud to report that the city of Fresno in my congressional district is doing just that. In calling this fact to the attention of other Members, I am pleased to include at this point in the RECORD the text of a proclamation issued by Mayor Ted C. Wills of Fresno, Calif., officially designating the week of April 20, 1975, as "Armenian Heritage Week."

PROCLAMATION

Whereas, a significant segment of the population of the San Joaquin Valley is composed of the American people who have contributed to the progress and betterment of life through agriculture, commerce, teaching, the professions, churches, and community organizations; and

Whereas, the Armenians among us are a remnant people of a nation against whom the first genocide of the 20th century was made, beginning on April 24, 1915, when a million and a half of them, comprising half the total of Armenians living during the Ottoman Empire, were annihilated by the Turkish government through a series of well-planned and secretly instituted atrocities, including the murder of the menfolk and the forced marches into the deserts of the women and children, where their ranks were decimated by hunger, lack of water and shelter; and

Whereas, by their own resolute Christian faith and will to survive and live again, and the generosity of many in the United States of America resulting in relief operations, a fraction of them were rescued and subsequently immigrated to this country and now comprise several hundred thousand in number; and

Whereas, their contribution to the building of America is evident by their leadership in the fields of education, science, medicine, the arts and government; and

Whereas, the Armenian community is an integral and important member of this multi-ethnic city and desires to help create and promote a greater appreciation for each culture; and

Whereas, we join the Armenians on this, the 60th Anniversary of this genocide, to affirm our conviction that genocide in whatever form and against whomever it is perpetrated, is rejected and condemned by us and all peace-loving and justice-seeking people of the world:

Now, therefore, I, Ted C. Wills, Mayor of the City of Fresno, do hereby proclaim the week of April 20-26, 1975, as Armenian Heritage Week and Thursday, April 24th as "Day of Remembrance of Man's Inhumanity to Man," and urge all the citizens of Fresno to render proper recognition to this solemn occasion and commemoration of the 60th Anniversary of the martyrdom of the Armenian people, and to participate in the activities of Armenian Heritage week.

ARMENIAN MARTYRS DAY IN NEW YORK STATE
AND NEW YORK CITY
1975

April 24, 1975 — marking the 60th
anniversary of the massacre of the
Armenians by the Turkish authori-
ties — was proclaimed "Armenian
Martyr's Day" by both the State of
New York and the City of New York.
The following are the proclamations
adapted by the New York State Legis-
lature, by New York State's Governor
Hugh L. Carey and by New York City's
Mayor Abraham D. Beame.

Source: A Heroic Posterity, New York
Prelacy of the Armenian Apotolic
Church, 1976.

A Heroic Posterity

PROCLAMATION

OFFICE OF THE MAYOR

CITY OF NEW YORK

The Twentieth Century has witnessed such violence, genocide, and disregard for human rights, as to cause concern for the future of human society. It began with the massacres that brought death to over one and one-half million Armenians living in Ottoman Turkey in 1915. In the decades that followed, many other peoples suffered tragedies, while violence continues rampant in our own decade around the world.

Sixty years have passed since that first genocide of 1915. Against this background, it is particularly significant that the Armenian Churches of America have chosen to make the April 1975 memorial observances the occasion for promoting world concern for the rights of all peoples. Through the inspiration of their own tragedies, major religious institutions have joined to determine how religious influences can be made stronger deterrent to mass aggression than has been possible in the past.

Now, therefore, I, Abraham D. Beame, in recognition of the importance of these events and activities for the future of human society, declare April 24, 1975 as

"A DAY OF MEMORY AND OF DEDICATION TO HUMAN RIGHTS."

We urge that there be given due attention and support to these efforts, to the end that our own nation shall continue to promote the cause of justice and of human rights for all peoples.

IN WITNESS WHEREOF I HAVE HEREUNTO
SET MY HAND AND CAUSED THE SEAL OF
THE CITY OF NEW YORK TO BE AFFIXED.

(Signed) Abraham D. Beame
Mayor, the City of New York

A Heroic Posterity

PROCLAMATION

STATE OF NEW YORK

Executive Chamber

Sixty years ago, millions of Armenians fled in terror from their ancient homeland, and one and a half million Armenians were massacred.

The world was shocked for it was seen as a deliberate attempt to exterminate the Armenian race.

On April 24th, Armenians the world over commemorate Martyrs' Day. It was on that day in 1915 when the Ottoman Turks arrested and killed 250 Armenian community leaders and intellectuals — an act which signaled the terrible events that followed.

All New Yorkers join our fellow citizens of Armenian heritage in honoring the memory of those martyrs in the hope that the conscience of the world can bring a halt to senseless slaughter, an end to all human suffering, and a reawakening of the sense of justice.

Let us pay tribute also to the survivors of the Armenian tragedy, especially to the hundreds of thousands who have made this country their home and have become hard-working, loyal citizens.

NOW, THEREFORE, I, Hugh L. Carey, Governor of the State of New York, do hereby proclaim April 24, 1975, as

ARMENIAN MARTYRS' DAY

in New York State.

GIVEN under my hand and the Privy Seal of the State at the Capitol in the City of Albany this fifteenth day of April in the year of our Lord one thousand nine hundred and seventy-five.

BY THE GOVERNOR:

(Signed) Hugh L. Carey

ARMENIAN MARTYRS DAY IN NEW JERSEY
1975

April 24, 1975 was proclaimed "Armenian Martyr's Day" by the State of New
Jersey's General Assembly, and by Governor Brendan Byrne. Both proclamations
are reproduced.

Source: A Heroic Posterity, New York:
Prelacy of the Armenian Apotolic
Church.

A Heroic Posterity

STATE OF NEW JERSEY

Executive Department

PROCLAMATION

WHEREAS, two hundred years ago, our nation committed itself to oppose tyranny and oppression, and began its historic struggle for independence; and

WHEREAS, that struggle has given hope and inspiration to millions of victims of persecution and oppression all over the world, many of whom have found refuge in our country; and

WHEREAS, sixty years ago, millions of Armenians fled in terror from their ancient homeland, and one and a half million Armenians were massacred in an attempt by the Turkish authorities of that time to exterminate the Armenian race; and

WHEREAS, on April 24, Armenians the world over commemorate Martyrs' Day, the day in 1915 when the Turks arrested and killed 250 Armenian community leaders and intellectuals; and

WHEREAS, it is fitting to honor the memory of those martyrs, in the hope that the conscience of the world can bring a halt to senseless slaughter, an end to all human suffering, and a reawakening of a sense of justice for the Armenian people; and

WHEREAS, it is also appropriate to pay tribute to the survivors of the Armenian tragedy, especially to the hundreds of thousands who have made their home in our country and have become hard-working, loyal citizens, many of whom we are proud to have reside in our own State of New Jersey;

NOW, THEREFORE, I, BRENDAN BYRNE, Governor of the State of New Jersey, do
hereby proclaim

APRIL 24, 1975

as

ARMENIAN MARTYRS DAY

in New Jersey, and urge all citizens to duly support its observance, for we must never be
indifferent, never forget, never ignore injustice and human suffering.

GIVEN, under my hand and the Great Seal of the State of New Jersey, this fourteenth day
of April in the year of Our Lord one thousand nine hundred and seventy-five, and in the
Independence of the United States, the one hundred and ninety-ninth.

(Signed) Brendan Byrne
Governor

A Heroic Posterity

STATE OF NEW JERSEY

GENERAL ASSEMBLY

State House, Trenton, N.J.

ASSEMBLY RESOLUTION
by Assemblyman Klein
Adopted April 7, 1975

WHEREAS, April 24, 1975, marks the 60th Anniversary of the launching of a systematic
genocide whereby between 1,500,000 and 2,000,000 Armenians dwelling in Turkey were
exterminated between 1915 and 1918; and,

WHEREAS, The history of the Armenian people, who through the ages have suffered
repeated subjugation and persecution by more powerful nations, from ancient Persia and
Rome to modern Turkey and Russia, is emblematic of the frequent recrudescences of
inhumanity which have from time to time threatened the stability of world civilization; and,

WHEREAS, There is currently pending in the Congress of the United States legislation
(House Joint Resolution 148) to designate April 24, 1975 as a "National Day of
Remembrance of Man's Inhumanity to Man"; now, therefore,

Be It Resolved by the General Assembly of the State of New Jersey:

That April 24, 1975, is hereby designated as a "Day of Remembrance of Man's Inhumanity
to Man" in this State, and the Governor is hereby requested to issue his proclamation
calling on the people of New Jersey to observe such day as a day of remembrance for all
the victims of genocide, especially those of Armenian ancestry who succumbed to .the
genocide perpetrated in Turkey in 1915-18, and in whose memory this date is
commemorated by all Armenians and their friends throughout the world.

THE ARMENIAN GENERAL BENEVOLENT UNION
OF AMERICA
1975 - 1976

The Armenian General Benevolent Union
of America, one of the largest Armenian American organizations, presents
a record of outstanding achievements
in the fields of national heritage
preservation, charity, education,
cultural activities and others. The
following are excerpts from the annual report for 1975-1976.

Source: Armenian General Benevolent
Union of America, Inc. Annual Report
1975-1976.

B. SCHOOLS

1. DETROIT

The AGBU Alex Manoogian School, currently in its seventh year of operation, provides
for the educational needs of 250 students in Kindergarten through 10th grade. This record enrollment is an increase of thirty percent from
1974-75 school year, keeping pace with the increased enrollment, the teaching staff has also
been increased to fourteen teachers. In addition
the school now employs a counselor and a librar-
ian.

The school plant currently includes   two
science laboratories, a library-media center, one
art room, one music room, one commercial course
room, a multi-purpose room, a home economics
room, and a gymnasium along with the academic
subject area classrooms.

Characterized by small classes and a teacher-
pupil ratio of one to sixteen, the students are
grouped so that high achievers may be challeng-
ed to their capacity and expectation level.

The small classes, furthermore, allow individual attention, independent study, and a balanc-
ed college preparatory program.

The school provides a diversified and balanc-
ed program of extra-curricular activities designed to make a positive contribution to the educational, social, and moral development of each
student. The program includes intramural and
interscholastic sports, a choral group, a dance en-

semble, student government, publications, dramatic groups, a Junior AGBU, honor society and orchestra.

The Manoogian School, its philosophy and curriculum have all been approved and accepted by the Michigan Department of Education, the Michigan Independent Schools Association, and the Independent Schools Association of the Central States.

Accreditation of the secondary school by the North Central Association of Secondary Schools and the University of Michigan will be commensurate with the establishment of the twelfth grade in 1977.

It is hoped that a 12th grade class will be opened next year, when the school will become a full secondary school, with 13 grades, covering the Kindergarten, the elementary classes, and the junior high and senior high cycles.

2. WATERTOWN

The AGBU Watertown School completed successfully its fifth year in June 1975 with 72 pupils. It's year-end exercises were held June 12, 1975 at the Cultural Hall of St. James Church in the presence of a large number of guests made of the childrens' parents and family friends. The children not only recited both in fluent Armenian and English and danced Armenian folk dances in colorful ethnic costumes but also presented "Vartan's Farm", a children's comedy.

Wednesday, September 3rd marked the beginning of the sixth school year. The year began with two additional classes and the number of pupils rose to 92, all regular students. The school moved to the former Sacred Heart School Building which has first class school facilities and takes much better care of the growing needs of our school.

Prof. Helen Vaznaian continued her valuable services as honorary principal of the school with Mrs. Stella Boy and Mrs. Rose Dirhem forming the school's advisory board while Hagop Atamian continued as its co-ordinator. The full-time teachers of the school were Mrs. Astghig Khatcadourian, Miss Deborah Kazanjian, Mrs. Sandra Agababian, Mrs. Cynthia Tanikleff, Miss Joan Hovnan and Miss Faith Spencer.

3. *AGBU Valley School* was officially in-

augurated on Sunday, February 1, 1976 amid
extensive ceremonies. The school which will be
under the joint auspices of the Western Diocese
and the AGBU Western District will be known
as the St. Peter-AGBU Armenian School.

The school has at present two classes, a kindergarten class and a first grade. It has nineteen
registered pupils. ages two to seven. The teachers
are Miss Sona Vartabedian and Mrs. Noemi Minasian.

C. YOUTH ACTIVITIES

The AGBU youth activities has gathered
strength and has registered a number of successes
both in its development program and scope of
activities. Two new youth chapters have been
given charters by the Central Committee, one for
the newly formed AGBU Richmond Chapter and
the other for the Fresno Youth.

During 1976 the AGBU National Youth Association has held four seminars, March, May,
September. 1975 and January 1976 where issues
effecting the whole movement were thrashed and
new policies adopted.

The AGBU Youth brought their support to
the fund-raising effort for Lebanon, conducted
throughout the U.S.A. by appeals through the
mail and also through some specific activities
such as the "No Dance Dance". The youth donat-
ed their monies without going to a ball and all
the money going to Lebanon. Their target for
America is $10,000.

New York — Our young people in New York
have finally a club room they can call their own.
The Vartan Hall in the Diocesan Complex has
been converted into a beautiful lounge and every
Friday evening a social entertainment is provided in the Hall or just a night of get together for
fellowship and indoor games.

SONG AND DANCE ENSEMBLES

Antranig — Regular rehearsals were held under the direction of Seta Kantarjian and the group
performed with notable success at the One World
Festival during September 1975 and also brought
its participation at other major ethnic dance fes-
tivals.

Ararat — Philedelphia: This dance group has fifty dancers and has held regular rehearsals under John Samelian and Tom Torkomian. The Ararat Dance Ensemble performed at "A Super Sunday-the American Way" an ethnic program attended by a million people, and on April 24, 1976 at the Philadelphia Folk Fair also attended by a very large audience.

The Ararat Choral Ensemble has a total of 40 members and is directed by Mr. George Suny. The choral group is rehearsing regularly for the upcoming Robin Hood Dell Concert.

Vahakn — Detroit: The Vahakn Dance Ensemble resumed rehearsals and has been practicing under the direction of Hairabed Kazazian. A performance is planned in the near future. The chairman of the group is Mrs. Paulette Apkarian.

Daron — Boston: The Daron Dance Ensemble is extremely active and is instructed by Miss Vicky Dilsizian. The chairman of the group is Mr. Zareh Mahserejian. The group practices every Sunday from 6:00 to 9:00 p.m. Activities and performances of the group were as follows:

March 1975 — performance at International Institute Ball

March 1975 — Daron Dance Ensemble Open House

April 1975 — performance for 60th Commemoration of the Armenian Martyrs

Jan. 1976 — Daron Dance Ensemble Open House

March 1976 — performed at Fund Raising Dinner for Lebanon

March 1976 — performed at International Institute Consulate Night

July 1976 — will perform at Robin Hood Dell Concert, Philadelphia

Daron Juniors: The Daron Juniors is a group of young people from 9-15 years of age who are holding practice sessions every Sunday from 5-6 p.m. There are 15 active members in this group and every week they are learning new dances and dance steps. This group will be a preparatory group for those who will eventually be members of the regular Daron Dance Ensemble. The group hopes to perform in the near future.

Sardarabad — Los Angeles: The Sardarabad Dance Ensemble has been practicing regularly under the direction of its instructors Mr. Varoujan Torikian, Ms. Arda Melkonian, and Mr. Edward Andonian. Also, Mr. Alexander Kazarianz gave his time and experience to the group, and Mr. Edward Hosharian once again offered his talents to the ensemble in the capacity of musical advisor. The Sardarabad Dance Ensemble will be performing at the 62nd National Convention of the AGBU in Los Angeles.

Sevag — Richmond: This is the newest dance ensemble group formed during 1975. The Philadelphia Youth Chapter was instrumental at the formation of this new group who have been active in the small Armenian community of Richmond.

ARMENIAN FOLK DANCE INSTRUCTION FOR CHILDREN

This past year two members of the Antranig Dance Ensemble have given their time and experience on Saturday mornings to two area Armenian schools. Mrs. Seta Kantarjian taught dance to the St. Gregorys Church Armenian School students, and Ms. Silva Kantarjian taught dance to the Holy Martyrs Church Armenian School Students.

AGBU DRAMA GROUP — BOSTON

The newly formed Hagop Baronian Drama Group under the leadership of Mr. Levon Agasyan is meeting regularly at the AGBU Center. There are approximately thirty regular members and the group is working hard as they will be performing for the public in the fall. The group is rehearsing for the performance of "Medzabadiv Mouratzganner" a musical comedy by Hagop Baronian. The cast is a very talented and enthusiastic group and is looking forward to a strong and successful performance.

SPORTS

Tennis and basketball continue to be two sports that are being promoted by our various youth groups and chapters. The Hye Tennis Set in New Jersey has 32 members and meets once a week, fifteen weeks during the summer enjoying the use of seven indoor courts.

Basketball however holds greater interest. The AGBU basketball teams in New York, New Jersey, Detroit, Boston, Los Angeles and Chicago participate in many tournaments and friendly matches in their home towns as well as nationally.

D. CAMPS

Camp Nubar — New York: A total of one hundred and eighty children enjoyed the camp this year. The greatest number, eighty-two children came for a two week period, fifty-six children came for a whole month. Twelve children came for a month but later extended their stay to six weeks while a total of thirty children remained the whole camping season of eight weeks.

The camp staff numbered sixty-two persons this summer, with Richard Tashjian as the Camp Director. The Camp Committee under the chairmanship of Daniel Kurkjian rendered valuable services not only during the two summer months but through the entire year.

Camp Ararat — Michigan: Camp Ararat had also a more active year. The 1975 camping season had three two weeks periods with forty-six campers participating at each period. This reflected an increase of twenty children over the past. A new activity in 1975 was horseback riding, proved very popular. This year greater stress was put on the study of the Armenian language with a special text especially prepared for the camper.

Very popular at Camp Ararat are the Barbecue days, when large numbers of campers' parents and AGBU members and friends visit the camp.

E. SCHOLARSHIP PROGRAM

In 1975 the AGBU Scholarship Committee of the Central Committee made 155 interest-free loans. The total amount loaned this year was $40,425. A total of 22 outright grants, amounting to $12,050 were awarded to unusually meritorious students.

From the inception of this program in 1954 through the scholastic year 1975, 2,048 scholarship recipients received loans aggregating $455,680. Of these students 171 are still studying ($132,300); of the balance 176 students have repaid their loans in full ($114,952); 16 have been delinquent ($10,050); 51 are untraceable ($28,800): repayment of loans from 90 former students have amounted to an unprecedented $20,678; 155 have just become due for repayment of $104,015 loaned to them.

In addition to the interest-free loans which become due for repayment after graduation, the Scholarship Committee awards a number of outright grants which AGBU friends and benefactors have established for the benefit of Armenians in the United States. Deserving students are chosen for these grants from among the loan applicants.

Haig and Haigouhi Kashian Fund	$ 1,000
Melkon Aijian Fund	1,000
Dikran Missirlian Fund	500
George Holopigian Fund	4,500
Harry Katcherian Fund	500
Aram Mendikian Fund	250
Meguerdich Sanossian Award	250

It is gratifying to note that some new additional grants are available for the benefit of the students. In 1976 two new grants were added:

Stephen H. Matthews Fund	$ 2,000
Manuel Serimian Fund	500

The following special grants are available to students who qualify:

Puzant Beshgeturian Award $ 3,000

Awarded to a student at Harvard University working toward an advanced degree in Armenian Studies.

Puzant Beshgeturian Award $ 2,000

For an MIT students to assist in tuition costs.

Walter Vartan - G. Ohanian Award $ 1,000

Established to assist a student during the freshman year in college.

Arshague & Evelyn
Toprahanian Awards $ 2,000

Two awards of $1,000 each for students from the West Coast.

Makrouhi Jedidian Award $ 600

Haigaz Tomboulian Awards two at $350 each
These awards are for students from overseas.

Hagop Topalian Award $ 600
Established to assist a student of Dikrana-
gerd origin.

Alan Fenner Award $ 300

N. Boyajian Award $ 300
These memorial awards are to assist students
attending law schools.

Adom Ourian Award $ 500
This award is established to assist a student
attending medical school.

Leon Sanossian Award $ 250
This award is established to assist a student
in the field of education.

Diran Patapanian Award $ 500
This grant is established to assist students
attending trade schools.

Gregory Deragopian Award $ 300
This memorial award is established to assist
a student in the field of aeronautics.

We are happy to report that the AGBU Fort
Lauderdale Chapter has helped the organization's
loan program by providing $1,000 a year for two
students from the Florida area.

F. ARMENIAN STUDIES

The AGBU accepts the encouragement of Armenian Studies in the United States as one of its
special missions. Programs of Armenian Studies
have always been accorded the support of the

Central Committee of America.

In New York, adult classes in Armenian for
beginners and advanced students had the highest
registration ever and students were instructed in
the Armenian language as well as in Armenian
history, art and culture.

In Fresno almost a regular school program
was conducted by the AGBU. The evening school
which began on March 3, 1975, with 75 students
reached a most-heartening figure of 151 as the
courses continued through two semesters.

The Armenian lessons were given at four

levels to adults and three levels to children. There were also classes in Armenian history and Armenian culture as well as a class for Armenian cooking and another for Armenian folk dancing.

San Diego chapter also promoted Armenian classes for adults as well as youngsters. Classes were offered in Armenian history and Armenian language. There was an Armenian conversation class for adults.

In New England, the Boston Youth Chapter organized an Armenian conversation class at the AGBU New England Center, which met every Thursday from 8:00 to 9:00 p. m.

In Providence adult Armenian classes continued once a week, Tuesdays 7-9:30 p.m. for beginners and advanced students.

Armenian classes continued to be offered both at Washington, D. C. and at San Jose, Ca.

In the Midwest there was substantial progress in the four Armenian part-time schools teaching the Armenian language, history and dance. Classes were located in Chicago, Cleveland, South Milwaukee and Waukegan.

In Watertown, for the fifth year, Armenian was taught in the public schools during 1975 as a second language in two grades, an hour a day. The total number of participating students was 45.

In the Belmont public school, for the fourth year, 20 Armenian children took Armenian as a second language. Courses continued also at Arlington, Mass. and San Fernando Valley in the California public schools with twenty-two children taking part.

As in previous years, the AGBU provided substantial financial assistance to the Armenian Studies programs at Columbia, Wayne and Massachusetts Universities.

B. PUBLICATIONS

To our knowledge no other Armenian organization in the United States of America has as many newsletters, bulletins and publications as the AGBU does. For besides our literary "Ararat Quarterly" and the Union's Bi-weekly organ "Hoosharar" various AGBU bodies publish a host of periodicals and newsletters such as:

a. The AGBU Torch, Los Angeles

b. Armenian Newsletter, San Diego

c. "Ani" Newsletter, Boston Youth

d. AGBU Newsletter, Rochester, N. Y.

e. Erepouni, AGBU Alex Manoogian School

f. Dziadzan, Sanoutz Association

g. Lradou, Detroit Intermediates

h. AGBU Newsletter, Detroit Ladies

1. HOOSHARAR — Owing to increasing costs and budgetary restrictions, efforts were made to reduce, so far as possible, the volume of each issue. However, care was taken to give as much space to the activities of our senior and youth chapters and other items of special interest to our readers.

The number of member and non-member subscribers is unchanged.

2. ARARAT — The editors are proud of the four most recent issues. The spring 1975 issue, illustrated by Marcel Apkarian, contained short stories by Marjorie Keyishian and Suzanne Zavrian and a fascinating description of Calouste Gulbenkian's fabulous museum in Lisbon containing some of the world's greatest paintings (Angele and Dickran Koumjian). Margueritte Bro contributed an eye-witness account of the Easter services in Jerusalem as celebrated by all faiths, emphasizing the role of the Armenian Church in the three-day event. The poetry section was particularly rich and the usual number of incisive book reviews rounded out the issue.

The summer 1975 issue contained a long, detailed chronicle by Paul Blaum of the Byzantine betrayal of the Armenian civilization and a provocative piece on the necessity of political activism by Leon Chorbajian, a sociologist at Lowell State University. Dr. H. Kelikian portrayed Armenian life in Immigrant America in a short story called "Crossroads". Among the poets represented were Harold Bond, Peter Balakian, Archie Minasian, Sayat Nova, and Alice Ezegelyan.

The autumn 1975 number was the 16th anniversary issue of ARARAT. Three stories, by Hindy Schacter, Peter Sourian, and Aram Saroyan (the latter two pieces from novels) provided an unusual offering of fiction. Richard Hovannisian's article threw light on the dimensions of democracy and authority in Caucasian Armenia of 1917-1919 and P. K. Thomajan wrote tou-

chingly of his boyhood experience with the Armenian church in "Keeping the Faith". There
was also a testament on the importance of art in
our lives by Martiros Saryan and an illustrated
appreciation of his work by Shahan Khachatrian.
Mary Matossian Morabito paid tribute to her
cousin Peter, an artist who lives and works in
San Diego. The article was illustrated by a mon-
tage of his work prepared by the artist for the
issue, Paul Sagsoorian (who also did the art for
the summer issue).

The issue contained thirteen reviews of books
by Armenians, a reflection of the intellectual fer-
ment that is taking place among Armenian-Americans during the seventies.

The winter 1976 issue, with a cover show-
ing a photograph of Armenian children who were
later victims of the massacre, was enlivened by
76 salty proverbs from Armenia compiled by Garig Basmadjian, a writer living in Paris, Ara Ba-
liozian's three informal essays: a long, authentic,
and moving account of the Turkish massacres by
a survivor, Perlanty Cherkezian! and an article
on Armenia's contribution to Gothic architecture
by Haroutune Kalayan of AUB's faculty. In the
area of fiction, there was a story by Robert Hew-
sen and another by Yeghishe Avedissian, each
about the intracacies of love among the Armenians in the Middle East. Among the poets contributing to this issue were Michael Depoian
(Casey), Peter Manuelian, Bedros Tourian, Ge-
vorg Emin, and Konstantinos Lardas. Mimi She-
raton of the *New York Times* reviewed Alice
Antreassian's new cookbook. Arthur Apissomian
created unusual graphic effects for the issue. For
the following year, one issue will be devoted to
the writers martyred in 1915 and one issue will
be a 100-page bi-centennial issue devoted to the
Armenian presence in America.

While the editor, Leo Hamalian, was in Iran
lecturing on a Fullbright grant, Harold Bond ca-
pably assumed many of the continuing duties of
the editor.

C. BOOKS

No new books were published during 1975,
although several have been considered but none
answered the criteria qualifying its publication.

In March 1975, Michael Arlen's book "Passage to Ararat" appeared in a serial form in the
New Yorker magazine. The appreciation of the

Armenian public was spontaneous and immediate. The AGBU Central Committee was the first to approach the publishers with large orders of the published book to make it available to members and friends of the Association. The book which hit the best seller's list was chosen by the National Book Awards as the best contemporary affairs book. In the short period of three months some 2,000 copies of the book were sold by the AGBU offices.

PRESIDENT GERALD FORD LAUDS ARMENIAN
AMERICAN CONTRIBUTIONS
1976

On April 5, 1976, President Gerald
Ford sent a special message to the
Armenian American community of Massachusetts, stressing the contributions made by Armenian Americans
during the two centuries of America's existence. The following is
the text of the message.

Source: <u>Kir</u> <u>Ou</u> <u>Kirk</u> (Letter and
Literature) vol. XX No. 21, 1976.

THE WHITE HOUSE

WASHINGTON

April 5, 1976

We now mark the beginning of our Third
Century as an Independent Nation as well
as the 200th Anniversary of the American
Revolution. For two centuries our Nation
has grown, changed and flourished. A
diverse people, drawn from all corners of
the earth, have joined together to fulfill
the promise of democracy.

America's Bicentennial is rich in history
and in the promise and potential of the
years that lie ahead. It is about the
events of our past, our achievements, our
traditions, our diversity, our freedoms,
our form of government and our continuing
commitment to a better life for all Americans. The Bicentennial offers each of us-
the opportunity to join with our fellow
citizens in honoring the past and preparing
for the future in communities across the
Nation. Thus, in joining together as races,
nationalities, and individuals, we also re-
tain and strengthen our traditions, background and personal freedom.

As we lay the cornerstone of America's
Third Century, I am most happy to commend
the members of the Armenian-American Community of the Commonwealth of Massachusetts
on their commemoration of our Nation's 200th
Anniversary. I welcome this opportunity to
honor their important contribution to the
history of our country and the vitality of
our way of life. Special Bicentennial programs such as this are helping to make our
great national celebration a memorable and
meaningful one for all.

Gerald R. Ford

ARMENIAN ACADEMICS IN THE UNITED STATES
1976

The Armenian Assembly, an organization representing the Armenian Americans regardless of their political or religious affiliations, published a Directory of Armenian American academic personnel. It was prepared on the basis of a three year study, and it revealed, among others, the following aspects.

Source: <u>Kir</u> <u>Ou</u> <u>Kirk</u> (Letter and Literature), vol. XX No. 21, 1976.

The Armenian Assembly's recently published Directory of Armenian academic personnel in the United States reveals that there are approximately 1,500 Armenian academics in America. This figure was arrived at by a three-year study which involved searching over 3,600 college catalogues-- 2,200 of which represented colleges and universities with graduate and professional programs, 1,130 of which represented two-year institutions, 170 law schools, and 116 medical schools.

A second technique used to find these individuals was to consult academic directories and the "lists" of professional societies. Once the names were compiled, those identified were sent a biographical questionnaire to gather the material needed for the publication.

The questionnaire provided information on the individual's rank, titles, address of institution where employed, degrees, dates granted and institutions from which they were received. While not all of those contacted sent back the material, the Directory is remarkably complete for a work of its type, and it represents the single unified source on Armenian faculty in North America.

The study further reveals that Armenians are strongly represented in the academic professions. Academic persons make up some .21% of the general population, while Armenian academics are some .33% of the total number of Armenians in America. This means that Armenians are 30% more heavily represented in the academic fields than the general American population.

The Directory contains a Geographic Distribution Table which shows that the heaviest concentration of Armenian scholars is in the Northeast with some 565 persons (45% of the total of Armenian scholars in America), followed by the West, 275 (22%), and the Mid-West, 254 (20%). The Southeast has 50 (4%), and Canada has 48 (3.8%).

DEMOGRAPHICS

These figures seem to show that Armenian academics tend to be where the Armenian population is the heaviest. But it must be kept in mind that Armenians have tended to settle in the large, populous centers of the U.S. where the largest numbers of educational institutions are located.

The study shows that in terms of individual states, California leads with some 243 individuals (19.4% of the total number of Armenians in the academic professions), followed by New York with 209 (16.7%), Massachusetts with 186 (15%), Michigan with 62 (5%), and Illinois with 59 (4.7%). This state by state approach shows that with the exception of Pennsylvania, with a heavy concentration of Armenians in Philadelphia, the states with the largest numbers of Armenians are those states with the highest number of Armenian academics.

Another way to look at these figures is to compare the number of Armenians teaching in each state to the total number of professional academics that are in those states. Since Armenian academics represent some .33% of the total academics in America, any state having a percentage of Armenian faculty larger than .33% of the total faculty is above average in Armenian representation. In this case we see that Massachusetts leads with 1.26%, followed by Rhode Island with 1.18%, California with .66%, Washington, D.C. with .62%, Connecticut with .57%, New York with .55%, New Jersey with .46%, Michigan with .42%, and Vermont with .36%. Here again we can see that Pennsylvania with .28% falls below the average.

If we look at the number of Armenians teaching in Connecticut and Vermont as extensions of the Armenian population of New York and Massachusetts, then the opinion that Armenian academics tend to be in the areas with the largest Armenian populations are in the chief centers of American higher education holds true with the exception of Pennsylvania.

The case of Pennsylvania would be closer to the norm if we include Washington, D.C. as an extension of the Armenian population of Philadelphia.

It is also interesting to note that since Armenians are some .19% of the total population, that any state with more than that percentage of the total academic population can be considered as "above average" in terms of its number of Armenian academics. Such states, in addition to the ones above, are: Illinois with .31%, Delaware with .30%, Maryland with .30%, Nevada with .30%, New Hampshire with .29%, Pennsylvania with .28%, North Dakota with .22%, Florida with .21%, and Indiana with .19%.

Copies of the Directory may be obtained for $3.00 (postage paid) through the office of the Armenian Assembly, 522 - 21st Street, N.W., Washington, D.C. 20006.

AN OPEN LETTER TO NEWLY ARRIVED ARMEN-
IAN IMMIGRANTS
1976

The author of the letter, Rev. Dr. G.
H. Chopourian, a prominent Armenian
American leader, centers on some dif-
ficulties faced by new Armenian immi-
grants and the characteristics of the
Armenian American community.

Source: <u>American Missionary Association of America News</u>, November 1976.

Welcome to the United States, land of liberty and mother of opportunity! Our communities greet you and *extend a warm hand of fellowship*. You have come to us from many parts of the world, each one for a particular reason. The *tragedies of Lebanon* is one such cause. Some of you have returned from Soviet Armenia after a residence of over a quarter century there—that is, you were "repatriated to Soviet Armenia" and "re-repatriated" to the U.S. There are others who come from other Soviet-dominated countries as well as Middle-Eastern lands.

You have your problems, of course.

You have before you the challenge to make adjustments to your new environment. These adjustments are numerous and encompass learning the ways of your neighbors, the traditions by which Americans live, social and economic and moral customs, transportation systems, schools and the English language. Some of you, who grew under strict communist regimes, in which personal freedoms were curtailed, will find it difficult to understand the relationship between freedom and responsibility as practised in the United States. Of course there are Americans who exploit freedom and act irresponsibly, but by and large the majority of Americans believe that freedom must be tempered with legislation and law. Some others will discover that Middle Eastern business techniques and attitudes will backfire as natives will not tolerate aggressive practices. Reactions of this and other kinds will create counter-reaction in you.

You will have to learn to make adjustments to your own counter-reactions, reminding yourself that in all probability you will conduct yourself like them in the not too distant future. To what other situations will you need to adjust yourself?

1. Most probably you will not find Armenian-Americans as strongly patriotic about Armenian matters as you are, and will be critical of them.

2. It is also possible that your own image of Armenians in the U.S. was much more favorable; you might find a larger number of Armenians are in the lower middle class than you realized; and you may be tempted to carry a chip on your shoulder.

3. You might also be asked humiliating questions of various kinds which will upset you for the inadequate image natives have of newcomers.

To these, too, you will need to adjust if you want your life to be one of good fellowship, friendship and happiness.

The native Armenians have their own problems.

They came to this country and worked, not only hard, but at very humiliating jobs in order to raise their economic and social status. There was a time when in some parts of this country an Armenian was not accepted to be a witness at court, was excluded from certain organizations and clubs, was considered to be a third class citizen. By hard labor, by strong ambition, by purposeful cooperation Armenians achieved an enviable standard and made a name for themselves as hardworking, honest, industrious, intelligent and wholesomely ambitious people. Armenian-Americans pride themselves in the fact that they occupy no less than second place among other minorities relative to the cleanest criminal records. As a result, they react strongly if newcomers disrupt in any way the social, moral, ethical and intellectual standards they have achieved. They consider themselves no less Armenian than anybody else and they do not wish newcomers to interprete their refusal to behave in a chauvinistic way as unpatriotic behavior.

Their problem, therefore, is their rejection of the newcomers' attitudes and their severe criticisms.

What is the answer? What solution can we find?

On the part of the newcomer, there needs to be an understanding of the Armenian-American citizen and his hopes and aspirations. They were among the early settlers in America and as immigrants did everything possible to preserve their culture and to adjust to American ways. They went to school, learned trades, engaged in commerce, built churches and schools, formed associations, published papers and created today's rather dynamic Armenian-American community. This is a remarkable achievement. They want to preserve this record and want your cooperation.

On the part of the Armenian-American citizen, there needs to be understanding of the needs of the newcomer and empathy for the newcomer's reactions. One of the important educational principles is that a person behaves in the way he has learnt to live. The newcomer has lived, worked, and engaged in commerce and activities in his own environment and has felt he was contributing to Armenian life intensely. Out here, in the U.S., he is homesick. The orange will not be as tasty here as in his own town, the olive will not be as tangy, the fig will not be as sweet, the pomegranate will not be as acid-flavored, the cucumber as crisp and friendship not as warm. The newcomer will not only need our sympathy, empathy and friendship, but our *objective understanding* of the needs of his spirit and of his *entire being*.

Together, let us keep up the Armenian spirit; even more, the Christian-Armenian spirit. Let us hold unto the good record we have established. Let us together aspire towards higher achievements in business, industry, the professions but even more so in conduct. Together let us build and raise the Armenian-American community to a *Number One* status among the minority groups in the United States. In a multi-cultural, multi-sectarian, pluralistic setting, with our culture, religion, and glorious past, let us prove to our neighbors in this world that we are a unique nation among the civilized nations of the world.

The Scriptures qualify the life of Christians as a concerned, loving and caring community as follows:

"But you are a chosen race, a royal priesthood, a dedicated nation, and a people claimed by God for his own, to proclaim the triumphs of him who has called you out of darkness into his marvellous light." 1 Peter 2:9.

The American-Armenian community is happy to have you here and willing to help in every way possible. It is only by unified efforts that we can achieve our goals. Come to us if you need guidance. Keeping our own standards high, it is important to accept American standards, benefit from the vast possibilities that the United States offers to us without misusing them. Speak Armenian, but learn how to speak English too. Fluency of language is important for best communication.

We are a royal and dedicated nation. Let us be a source of courage, hope and inspiration to the entire U.S. communities by means of self-elevating and edifying conduct. Let us demonstrate love and concern for fellow Armenians and, to repeat, LET US BE NUMBER ONE IN THE MINORITY GROUPS OF THE UNITED STATES.

ARMENIAN THANK YOU, AMERICA DAY IN NEW
                    YORK CITY
                      1976

On November 28, 1976, representatives
of Armenian Americans from all over
the United States acknowledged their
gratitude to America, and organized
a special "Thank You, America" banquet in New York City. The banquet
was attended by 1300 guests, and on
this occasion Mayor Abraham Beam's proclaimed November 28, 1976 as "Armenian
Thank You, America Day" in New York
City. The text of the proclamation
follows.

Source: The Armenian Reporter vol.
X, No. 6, December 2, 1976.

Mayor's Proclamation

Today the Armenian-American community is celebrating history
and making history, and it is a great pleasure for me to share this
occasion with all of you. There are many ways of saying thank you,
and many reasons why we do.

The Armenian community's magnificent gift of 21 treasured
tapestries to the city of New York is indeed a particularly generous,
beautiful, and unique expression of gratitude. The Herter tapestries
depict 17th and 18th century events in the city of New York. The
history of the collection as well as the scenes themselves, tell a
fascinating story, but the generous bequethal of them also adds
another illustrious chapter to the story of our national fabric which
itself is a tapestry woven with the contributions of all people.

And this tribute to the city of New York and the thank you to
America, is a tribute as well, to the Armenian heritage that has
enriched our land over the years.

The presentation of the tapestries gloriously extends the Armenian-American tradition of participation in our society. The art
world, the city of New York, all Americans and people from all
countries who will be able to see these tapestries in the Metropolitan
Museum owe the Armenian community many thank yous for this
very special thank you. And I want to express my appreciation to
John Korenian, to the Armenian Sisters Academy, and to the
honored guests and benefactors. With their help the tapestries have
come home to New York. And now on behalf of a grateful city I'm
happy to issue this proclamation designating today as Armenian
thank you day, thank you America day, and it reads as follows:

In this the year of America's Bicentennial it is fitting to reflect
upon what has made our country unique among nations. For over
200 years we have opened our doors to peoples from many lands
who have come here in the search for freedom. We in this country
and particularly our great city of New York have become a haven,
and in turn all of our lives have been enriched many-fold by
immigrants to this land. One of the people seeking freedom from

tyranny and poverty who came to these shores were the Armenians. Armenian-Americans have made great contributions to the arts, sciences and business and we are here to recognize and salute them. Their generosity in the returning to New York of 21 unique tapestries depicting various scenes from American history so that they may be displayed at museums and other public institutions for the appreciation of all New Yorkers is a gift most welcome and in keeping with the spirit of the Bicentennial. And so as mayor of this city it is my pleasure and privilege to proclaim Sunday, November 28, 1976 as Armenian thank you America day in New York City and ask all citizens to join in this endeavor.

PRESIDENT GERALD FORD'S MESSAGE TO THE
THANK YOU, AMERICA BANQUET
1976

On November 28, 1976, the Armenian American gathering at the "Thank You, America" banquet received the following
message from President Gerald Ford.

Source: The Armenian Reporter, vol X,
No. 6, December 2, 1976.

Message of President Ford

I welcome the opportunity of this Armenian American Day observance in New York City to express a
grateful nation's continuing pride in the contributions
of its citizens of Armenian
descent.

> During this Bicentennial
> year we are more than ever
> mindful of the strength and
> vitality we have derived from
> our diverse ancestral heritage,
> and it is especially ap-
> propriate that we join in
> tribute to the Armenian
> American community for
> perpetuating a legacy that has
> so greatly enriched our way
> of life.

I hope that this will be a happy and memorable
observance for all who participate.

PRESIDENT ELECT JIMMY CARTER'S MESSAGE
TO THE THANK YOU, AMERICA BANQUET
1976

On November 28, 1976, the Armenian
Americans assembled at the "Thank
You, America" banquet received the
following message from President
elect Jimmy Carter.

Source: The Armenian Observer, vol.
VI, No. 50, December 8, 1976

PRESIDENT—ELECT JIMMY CARTER'S TELEGRAM TO THE 'THANK YOU, AMERICA' BANQUET

It gives me great pleasure to salute the Armenian-American community on this unique occasion. That you have gathered expressly to thank America in this year of bicentennial celebration says much about the spirit of your people. That your thanks should be accompanied by an admirable gift of historical tapestries says much about the heart of your people. The extraordinary is often the product of ordinary but ¬otivated people. I cite particularly those who have been transposed from oppressions elsewhere to opportunity in America, once persecuted or deprived, now avid and appreciative of a new life, a new chance to learn and create and improve.

For evidence, look at your own history. Out of the depths of your experience and enterprise, a small people only in number, Armenians have contributed abundantly to the quality and dignity of America. Moreover, while you have retained your centuries old heritage and identity, you're wholly Americans. This is exemplary of America's myriad ethnic societies. A paradox is that we are stronger because of and not dispite of our diversity of origin, race, culture and creed. Hence, your gift of tapestries is far more than material. It is symbolic for we are many colors many motifs, vibrant and dynamic each clearly delineate, yet woven in harmony to form a single bold tapestry, precious beyond price.

Now, as we in peace enter our third century of freedom, may you continue to bless America even as America has blessed you.

Sincerely,
Jimmy Carter

THE TRADITIONAL ARMENIAN WEDDING
1976

A very interesting article by L. Vartanian sheds light on the traditional Armenian wedding as preserved during centuries till our day. Here are some relevant excerpts.

Source: The Armenian Reporter, December 23, 1976.

Almost until the first quarter of this century the Armenian folk wedding was preserved in all its tradition and was a picturesque and festive occasion. The wedding cycle as our grandfathers still remember it, took shape and was elaborated over the ages. Hence, it was quite natural for it to reflect the mores of bygone epochs, along with the oldest magic rites and rituals and even superstitions, aiming in the long run to secure the welfare and happiness of the young couple.

During the millennial history of the Armenian people common forms of material and spiritual culture have evolved and been passed on from one generation to another. However, in every historico-ethnographic region, both in East and West Armenia, this culture had its local, distinct forms - in dress, in ways of tilling the land, folk beliefs and house-building. However, in spite of certain differences in detail, the Armenian wedding rituals of various regions are essentially identical.

The whole complex mass of rituals can be divided up into a series of pre-wedding, wedding proper and post-wedding rituals, which succeed one another in a strictly set up order.

Among the Armenians, marriage was allowed between relatives not closer than the seventh degree of consanguinity. It happened though that marriage was occasionally effected between relatives with a fifth degree of consanguinity. Marriage between closer relations was allowed only in exceptional cases by a special permission of the Catholicos. Sometimes marriage was effected at the rather early ages of 10-14. Now and then children were betrothed from the cradle.

The mother of the young man looked for a bride, gathering information about her and her family. When it was time for the son to marry, it was ascertained through a matchmaker whether the proposal would be accepted. In a roundabout way the girl's mother would find out how her daughter felt about it, but quite often the consent of the couple, especially that of the girl, was not taken into consideration at all.

In the case of a positive reply, the bridegroom's parents and their closest relatives paid a visit to the girl's parents to hand over the token of the betrothal - neshan, a ringlet or a necklace, a locket, a chain with a pendant of coins. From that day on the girl was considered engaged. Neither the bride-to-be nor the bridegroom-to-be, for that matter, attended the engagement. Once the neshan was handed over, the two families became kinsmen by affinity and assisted each other in every possible way. On all feast days a khoncha on a salver - smeets, vodka and symbols of fertility and pomegranates or apples would be sent back and forth from the boy's house to the girl's house. At Easter a lamb would be sent to be butchered on the threshold of the betrothed girl's house as an Easter offering. Sometimes several years passed before the marriage took place.

SETTING THE DATE

Once the nuptial day was settled by consent of both parties, they fixed the number of guests, and a token sum meant for the bride's mother for having nourished the baby daughter at her breast (hence the term "breast fee"), as well as the extent of the dowry. The latter included the bed and bedding, the nuptial curtain, plates and dishes, sometimes cattle, the amount of various foodstuffs to be sent to the bride's house by the bridegroom's father for the wedding feast. The nuptial dress was sent to the bride by the bridegroom's relatives.

As a rule, the weddings took place in autumn or winter, after field work was over. In many regions of Armenia people preferred to arrange marriages at Shrovetide, during the days of the ancient and rather cherished feast connected with the cult of fertility and the reviving forces of nature. The wedding festivities lasted three days. Usually they started on Friday and ended on Sunday. Now and then the wedding would last seven days and nights.

One of the preliminary rites was the bathing of the bride by her relatives who brought along omelettes and honey. In some regions the bathing was accompanied with improvised songs. As to the bridegroom's bath, it was a more modest affair.

A merry animation and bustle reigned in the families of the young couple. In both houses the baking of bread was a solemn ritual. When sifting the flour and kneading the dough, they observed a time-honored order of actions. Handed over by the eldest woman, the sifted flour was passed on, till it reached the hands of the women especially called for this purpose. The houses were put in a spick and span order, especially the corner where the bride was to be seated behind the curtain. The curtain was ornamented with various amulets and stripes to protect the bride from evil eyes and evil spirits. At the bridegroom's house wine karafs were opened in the presence of elderly relatives and the pitchers brimmed over. The bridegroom's father accompanied by a priest, went to the cemetery where offices were held on the tombs of ancestors and all the deceased. In the company of the priest the bridegroom made the round of all the houses where a relative had died the previous year. In many regions the sponsor's wife drew stars on the ceiling, walls and table of the bridegroom's house, so that the new couple might live under "the blessings of stars".

BACHELOR PARTY

On the eve of the wedding the bridegroom invited his bachelor pals to a "lads' party" to elect his suite - bodyguard, dubbed *magar* in East Armenia and *azab* in West Armenia. The bridegroom's suite with its leader, *makarapet*, or *azabapet*, quite often mounted and armed, persistently accompanied the bridegroom and bride throughout the wedding cycle.

On Friday morning the *ganch* - the call of the pipes and drums from the roof of the bridegroom's house proclaimed the start of the wedding.

Hearing the sound of the pipe the children ran to the bridegroom's house from all the streets, inviting everybody they met to the wedding. If the bride was from another village, the youth barred the way of the in-laws who had come to take away the bride demanding a ransom.

In all the wedding ceremonies the leading part was played by the *kavor* (sponsor) and his wife *kavoraguin*. Then the *kavor* became godfather. The kavorship was passed on from one generation to another in the same family, this link being no less strong than blood relationship. As a most worthy and respectable person the *kavor* was especially invited to the wedding by the bridegroom's father or by one of the senior members of the family or clan.

The guests gathered in the bridegroom's house and started feasting with music, jokes, boisterous merrymaking. As a matter of fact throughout the wedding cycle there was no lack of rejoicing, games, singing, dancing. This happy atmosphere was considered a good omen for a lifelong marital companionship. Hence, the effort to celebrate it as festively as possible.

When the guests took leave, the bridegroom and the *kavor* or sponsor, escorted by the *jagars* and the musicians, and the butcher who took along the sheep meant for an offering, made for the bride's house. On the threshold of her house the sheep was slaughtered to the tune of the pipe and drum. The *kavor* dipped into the blood an unfastened lock or the blade of a knife and some thread. He knotted the thread, fastened the lock with the key and put the blade into the sheath.

A priest blesses the gifts.

APPENDICES

ARMENIAN AMERICAN INSTITUTIONS, ORGANIZATIONS AND FOUNDATIONS

AMERICAN NATIONAL COMMITTEE TO AID HOMELESS ARMENIANS
        240 Stockton Street
        San Francisco, California 94108

ARMENIAN ASSEMBLY
        55 Twenty First Street, N.W.
        Suite 120
        Washington, D.C. 20006

ARMENIAN APOSTOLIC CHURCH OF AMERICA
        138 East 39 Street
        New York, New York 10016

ARMENIAN CHURCH OF NORTH AMERICA
        Eastern Diocese
          St. Vartan Cathedral
          630 Second Avenue
          New York, New York 10016

        Diocese of California
          1201 North Vine Street
          Hollywood, Calif. 90038

ARMENIAN CHURCH YOUTH ORGANIZATION OF AMERICA
        630 Second Avenue
        New York, New York 10016

ARMENIAN EDUCATIONAL FOUNDATION
        5300 Santa Monica Boulevard
        Los Angeles, California 90029

ARMENIAN GENERAL BENEVOLENT UNION OF AMERICA
        628 Second Avenue
        New York, New York 10016

ARMENIAN LIBRARY AND MUSEUM OF AMERICA
        Post Office Box 147
        Belmont, Massachusetts 02178

ARMENIAN LITERARY SOCIETY
        114 First Street
        Yonkers, New York 10704

ARMENIAN MISSIONARY ASSOCIATION OF AMERICA
        140 Forest Avenue
        Paramus, New Jersey 07652

ARMENIAN PROGRESSIVE LEAGUE OF AMERICA
39 West 32nd Street
New York, New York

ARMENIAN RELIEF SOCIETY
212 Stuart Street
Boston, Massachusetts 02116

ARMENIAN REVOLUTIONARY FEDERATION OF AMERICA
212 Stuart Street
Boston, Massachusetts 02116

ARMENIAN SCIENTIFIC ASSOCIATION OF AMERICA
30 Half Moon Lane
Irvington, New York 10533

ARMENIAN STUDENTS ASSOCIATION OF AMERICA
GPO Box 1557
New York, New York 10001

ARMENIAN WOMEN's WELFARE ASSOCIATION
431 Pond Street
Jamaica Plain, Massachusetts 02130

ARMENIAN YOUTH FEDERATION OF AMERICA
304-A School Street
Watertown, Massachusetts 02172

ARS ETHNIC HERITAGE PROJECT
304 School Street
Watertown, Massachusetts 02178

BAIKAR ASSOCIATION
755 Mount Auburn Street
Watertown, Massachusetts 02172

FAMILIAN (ISADOR & SUNNY) FOUNDATION
9595 Wilshire Boulevard
Beverly Hills, California 90212

GULBENKIAN (GULLABI) FOUNDATION, INC.
630 Second Avenue
New York, New York 10016

HAIRENIK ASSOCIATION
212 Stuart Street
Boston, Massachusetts 02116

THE KARAGHEUSIAN COMMEMORATIVE CORPORATION
79 Madison Avenue
Room 904
New York, New York 10019

KEVORKIAN (HAGOP & MARJORIE) FOUNDATION, INC.
    1411 Third Avenue
    New York, New York 10028

MANOOGIAN (ALEX & MARIE) FOUNDATION
    500 Stephenson Highway
    Suite 410
    Troy, Michigan 48084

NATIONAL ASSOCIATION FOR ARMENIAN STUDIES AND RESEARCH
    175 Mt. Auburn Street
    Cambridge, Massachusetts

PHILIBOSIAN (STEPHEN) FOUNDATION
    Hill Top Farms
    Radnor, Pennsylvania 19087

APPENDICES
Armenian American Periodicals

ARMENIAN AMERICAN PERIODICALS

A.M.A.A. NEWS
The Armenian Missionary Asso.
of America, Inc.
   140 Forest Avenue
   Paramus, New Jersey 07652

ARARAT
Armenian General Benevolent
Union of America, Inc.
   628 Second Avenue
   New York, New York 10016

ARMENIAN CHURCH
Diocese of the Armenian Church
of America
   630 Second Avenue
   New York, New York 10016

ARMENIAN GUARDIAN
Armenian Church Youth Organization of America
   630 Second Avenue
   New York, New York 10016

THE ARMENIAN MIRROR-SPECTATOR
Baikar Association, Inc.
   755 Mount Auburn Street
   Watertown, Mass. 02172

ARMENIAN OBSERVER
   6646 Hollywood Boulevard
   Hollywood, Calif. 90028

THE ARMENIAN REPORTER
The Armenian Reporter, Inc.
   42-60 Main Street
   Flushing, New York 11355

THE ARMENIAN REVIEW
Hairenik Association
   212 Stuart Street
   Boston, Mass. 02116

ARMENIAN TIMES-URARTU
   38 West 32nd Street
   New York, New York 10001

THE ARMENIAN WEEKLY
Hairenik Association
   212 Stuart Street
   Boston, Mass. 02116

ASBAREZ
Armenian Revolutionary Federation
Central Committee of California
   1501 Venice Boulevard
   Los Angeles, Calif. 90006

BAIKAR
Baikar Association
   755 Mount Auburn Street
   Watertown, Mass. 02172

BARI LOUR
St. Peter Armenian Apostolic
Church
   17231 Sherman Way
   Van Nuys, Calif. 91406

BULLETIN OF THE ARMENIAN SCIEN-
TIFIC ASSOCIATION OF AMERICA
   30 Half Moon Lane
   Irvington, New York 10533

CALIFORNIA COURIER
   Post Office Box 966
   Fresno, Calif. 93714

GERMANIK
Union of Marash Armenians
   36-33 169th Street
   Flushing, New York 11358

HAIRENIK
Armenian Revolutionary Federation
of America
   212 Stuart Street
   Boston, Mass. 02116

HAI SIRD
Armenian Relief Society, Inc.
   212 Stuart Street
   Boston, Massachusetts 02116

HAYASTANYAITZ YEGEGHETZY
Diocese of the Armenian Church
of America
　630 Second Avenue
　New York, New York 10016

HOOSHARAR
Armenian General Benevolent
Union of America, Inc.
　628 Second Avenue
　New York, New York 10016

KILIKIA
Prelacy of the Armenian Apostolic
Church of America
　777 United Nations Plaza
　New York, New York 10017

KIR-OU-KIRK
Armenian Literary Society, Inc.
　114 First Street
　Yonkers, New York 10704

LOUSAROVICH
St. Gregory Illuminator Church
of Armenia
　630 Second Avenue
　New York, New York 10016

LRAPER
Armenian Progressive League of
America
　151 West 25th Street
　New York, N.Y. 10001

MAIR YEGEGHETZI
St. Illuminator's Armenian
Apostolic Church
　221 East 27th Street
　New York, New York 10016

THE MONTHLY BULLETIN
The Armenian Evangelical Church
of America
　152 East 34th Street
　New York, New York 10016

NOR ASHKAR WEEKLY
　151 West 25th Street
　New York, New York 10001

NOR OR
Nor Or Publishing Association
　5076 West Pico Boulevard
　Los Angeles, Calif. 90019

PAP OUKHTI
Educational Association of
Malatia
　12813 Gay Avenue
　Cleveland, Ohio 44105

P'AROS
St. Sahak and St. Mesrop Armenian Apostolic Church
　70 Jefferson Street
　Providence, Rhode Island 02908

SHOGHAKAT'
St. Grigor Lousarovitch Armenian
Apostolic Church
　2215 East Colorado Boulevard
　Pasadena, California 91107

SHOGHAKAT'
St. Sargis Armenian Apostolic
Church
　42nd Avenue at 213rd Street
　Bayside, New York 11361

YERITASARD HAYASTAN
Hunchakian Party of America
　Post Office Box 9
　Madison Square Garden
　New York, New York 10010

APPENDICES
Biographical Sketches of Prominent Armenian Americans

Biographical sketches of prominent Armenian Americans--recipients of the
BICENTENNIAL AWARD FOR EXCELLENCE

Lucine Amarda

Operaticarts — Soprano, Metropolitan Opera. An international luminary of opera, concert, screen, radio, television and recordings, Lucine Amara is agifted musician and linguist, who sings in 8 languages. With a repertoire of over thirty major operatic roles, Miss Amara was honored by the Met in November 1975, upon her 25th anniversary with that distinguished institution. On hearing her perform, violonist Issac Stern once remarked, "You sing like a beautiful violin." To which we add, "and like a beautiful Armenian-American of whom we are justly proud."

Emik A. Avakian

Science, Scientist, Engineer, Inventor, President of Avakian Systems Development. Among his contributions within the science of electronic communications, this remarkable inventor has given audible speech to the computer and introduced the tablet system of data entry, surpassing the indirect punch-card method. Author of scores of scientific papers and recipient of numerous awards and international honors, his main effort today is to aid communication within man's own body. Stricken by the breakdown of his own neurological system, Emik Avakian's goal is to augment faulty neuro mechanisms with a thimble-sized computer that would be permanently implanted in one's body.

Lili Chookasian

Operatic Arts - Contralto, Metropolitan Opera Co. Possessor of an extraordinary, sumptuous voice, described by the New York Times as "dark, rich... used with great sensitivity and power, feeling for musical phrase and projection." Lili Chookasian today ranks among the great contraltos in the world of opera, concert, and oratorio. Versatile as she is vivacious, Miss Chookasian's repertoire spans from the cantatas of Bach to Wagner's heroic "Ring" cycle - and still finds room for the whimsy of Hansel & Gretel. A gifted artist who has brought joy to music lovers everywhere, Lil Chookasian in private life is proud to be known as Mrs. George Gavejian and the mother of three children.

Mike Connors

Dramatic Arts - Actor. His incredible success as television's "Mannix" has won millions of fans in 80 countries and resulted in five Emmy nominations plus a Golden Globe award as Best Actor. At the very top of the fantastic though fragile world of show business, Mike Connors yet emerges as a magnetic and genuine person. Despite grueling 12 to 14 hour days on the Mannix set, his personal life is devoted to his family, his wife of more than 20 years, and to the support of such charities as the Armenian General Benevolent Union and the Arm. General Benevolent Union and the American Cancer Society. Ever the thorough professional throughout a glittering career in television and cinema, Mike Connors is the rare star in the Hollywood sky with his feet on the ground -- and his heart with his friends

Ernest H. Dervishian

In Service to His Country Attorney. By the time he retired from the United States Army in November, 1945 with the rank of Colonel, this recipient of a world War II battlefield commission hadwon a chestfull of decorations from Italy and Poland, as well as the United States. Above all, he, among a handful of men in American military history, was awarded this nation's supreme and highest citation, the Congressional Medal of Honor. Thus, a son of Armenian heritage brings honor to our name, symbolizing the highest qualities of loyalty, valor and sacrifice. Today, Ernest Herbert Dervishian carries these same qualities to his peaceful pursuits as a distinguished family-man and churchman, and honored leader of numerous professional and fraternal organizations -- not least of all, the Knights of Vartan.

Arlene Francis

Dramatic Arts - Actress. Bennett Cerf hailed Arlene Francis as the "Queen of Broadway." First Lady Betty Ford warmly commended her championship of women's rights. Clive Barnes wrote of her supreme naturalness, a comedienne of great talent and versatility. Ever young, ever glamorous, Arlene Francis gained international fame as the star of television's long-running "What's My Line," dazzling millions with her charm and with her quick incisive wit. Star of stage, screen and T.V., her philosophy remains simple and well worth emulating: Give your best and your potential will surprise you. The higher you reach, the higher you will go.

Khoren der Horootian

Fine Arts - Sculptor. The commencement of his outstanding career in the fine arts began with his escape to the United States from the tragic crucible of the 1915 Turkish massacres which claimed his priest father and brother. Thus Khoren Der Harootian's characteristics -- intensity, spirituality, strength, integrity -- are inevitably manifest in his work. Museums the world around, ranging from New York's mighty Metropolitan to the State Museum in Yerevan, have proudly displayed the sculptures of Khoren Der Harootian. And yet, the capstone of an honor-studded career of over half a century occurred only last week, Armenian Martyrs Day, at the Philadelphia Museum of Art: The dedication of his masterwork, "Meher" -- the enduring monument of thanks from all Armenian-Americans to the United States of America.

David Hedison

Dramatic Arts - Actor. With a list of credits that could fill a book, including award-winning roles in both the American and British stage and screen, David Hedison is perhaps best known as the exciting star of the long-running television series, "Voyage to the Bottom of the Sea." As scholarly as he is athletic and handsome, David Hedison is critically regarded as a versatile performer who communicates dramatically in every medium of acting. Like his great and good friend Mike Connors, David Hedison is a devoted family man and generous contributor of time and talent to numerous educational and charitable causes, particularly those affecting Armenian-Americans.

Alan Hovhaness

Music - Composer. One of America's most profound composers, Alan Hovhaness has achieved international appeal through his inventive fusing of Oriental source material and classical Western modes. Haunting, mysterious, deeply God-oriented, the work of Alan Hovhaness communicates the beauty and soul of Armenian culture to the four corners of the earth. By any serious measure, film "Becky Sharp," he has al-rank of composers of this century and his music is performed and recorded with equal appreciation in the East as well as in the West. Prolific in all forms of composition yet humbly reluctant to make any public show of his genius, Alan Hovhaness lets his music speak for him. His music will speak to the ages.

Hirair S. Hovnanian

Business and Industry - Builder. Builder extraordinaire, his concern for humanity is manifest in the fact that he is both a builder of cities and a builder of people through his many efforts in cultural, educational and civic endeavors. Two retirement communities, now nearing completion, embody Hirair Hovnanian's total involvement in furthering the best through his professional and personal interests. Representative of a new generation who came to America after World War II, he retains a strong respect for Armenian traditions and ideals - giving fully of himself to show the way for others - building for the future on the strong foundations of the past.

Harry A. Kuljian

Business and Industry - Founder, The Kuljian Corp. Though he is no longer with us, the benefits of this dynamic and inventive engineer's work are universal. Harry Kuljian brought the impact of electronic power to many millions of people in this nation and the under-developed countries of the world. In his book, "The Universe and its Man" he set forth his sadness in the fact that advances in human relations did not keep pace with the advance in technology. But his was not merely a voice crying in vain. His philanthropic efforts were as real and as powerful as the physical plants he built.

Rouben Maloulian

Cinematic Arts - Director, Producer, Writer. As a director, producer and writer, he has thrilled us at times, terrified us, but above all entertained us. From "Dr. Jeckyll and Mr. Hyde" to the first Technicolor film "Becky Sharp" he has always been an innovator. Rouben Mamoulian has blended the arts and sciences to bring us many hours of unforgettable entertainment. A great among greats, he has combined his talents with those of the world's outstanding artists in all the performing arts to widen our vision, delight our hearing, and touch the heart of all. Merely a listing of his many theatrical triumphs would immediately recall to the minds of all of us the emotional depths he probed. And to a new generation he has shown the way.

Edward Mardigian

Business and Industry - Engineer, Founder, Mardigian Corporation. Long a believer in the necessity of building bridges for understanding, he has devoted much of his life to this work. Edward Mardigian's diverse efforts in the business world are stamped with the hallmark of ringing success, as are his efforts to preserve our common heritage. Often called upon to express his conviction and devotion to Armenian cultural and educational institutions, in a recent address he stressed the national awakening of our Armenian-American youth to community goals and our religious and cultural calling. Through his many philanthropies in helping to build and maintain our institutions, Edward Mardigian has matched word with deed.

George Mardikian

Business and Industry Restaurateur, Patriot. Few people have earned as many colorful titles as the legendary George Mardikian: "San Francisco's Chopin of Chefs," "advisor to Presidents," and "Uncle Sam's No. 1 Fan" are but a few. Friend of legions of the humble and the exalted, this

irrepressible and big-hearted
man knows what it is to be both.
Among his numerous philanthropies as a proud Armenian-
American, one of his greatest
triumphs was the transplanting
of hundreds of displaced
Armenians to America's shores.
Recipient of an endless list of
tributes, no pacon of praise can
match the elocution of his words:
"The priceless thing America has
given me has nothing to do with
money or fame. I call it the
dignity of being American."

Alex Manoogian

Business and Industry -
Founder, Masco Corporation.
Before the age of 30 he established an industry. Throughout
his life, Mr. Manoogian's dedication to maintaining the Armenian
cultural heritage has found his
support of church and charity,
schools and sports, community
centers and cultural organizations throughout the nation and
the world. Distinguished president of the Armenian General
Benevolent Union International,
his philanthropic efforts have
included establishing AGBU
Centers through North and
South America, Europe and the
Middle East. An outstanding
product of the Armenian drive
for excellence, Alex Manoogian
has traversed the globe to foster
and enrich the Armenian heritage.

Stephen P. Mugar

Business and Industry -
Founder, Star Market Co.
Epithets such as democracy,
distinguished service, Americanism, and human relations catch
the eye as one encounters the
awards and honors granted this
pillar of American ideals and
opportunity. A large chain of
food markets attests to Stephen
Mugar's determination in the
business world. Moreover, his
presence, strength and guiding
hand are to be found in many

endeavors aimed at preserving
our Armenian Heritage. Trustee
of four colleges and universities,
Fellow at Brandeis University,
the recipient of five honorary
doctorate degrees -- all bear
evidence of his sure belief in the
American Dream.

Ara Parseghian

Athletics - Former Head Foot-
ball Coach, Notre Dame. When
the Notre Dame team lost for
four straight years to North-
western, the school fathers realized that the only way to stop the
streak was to hire the enemy
coach. His name: Ara Raoul
Paraseghian. For the next eleven
seasons, this dedicated and bril-
liant man transposed a losing
team into a disciplined band of
athletes who truly earned the
name -- Fighting Irish. When the
era of Ara closed, his record
spoke for itself: 95 wins, 17
losses, 5 ties. A head coach at 27,
Ara Parseghian earned the most
coveted awards of his profession
including "Coach of the Year."
Today, as a businessman, family-
man, churchman, gentleman,
and as chairman of the Multiple
Sclerosis Campaign, one trait
stands clear: In all things, Ara
Parseghian is a winner.

Stephen Philibosian

Business and Industry -
Entrepreneur, Philanthropist.
The saga of Stephen Philibosian
might be just one more tale of
rags to riches but for a vital
difference: This man gave his
riches to those who were in rags.
Notwithstanding his inborn
genius for salesmanship that
vaulted him from immigrant lad
to wealthy businessman,

Stephen Philibosian was above all a compassionate humanitarian. A non-stop motivator in a legion of Armenian and non-Armenian charities, his primary medium for philanthropy was the Armenian Missionary Association of America. Through this institutitution Stephen Philibosian became an inspiring practical force that bore such fruit as Haigazian College and the Child Education program, serving hundreds of orphans in the Middle East. Today, the man has gone home to God, but his magnanimous spirit and good works continue unabated through the Foundation that bears his name.

William Saroyan

Literary Arts - Writer. No matter what you know of this great man. perhaps nothing so fittingly catches his incorrigibly free spirit and joie de vivre as his recent remark, "I don't have to write plays for a living. I've got a bicycle." Can anyone not love William Saroyan? Can there be an Armenian anywhere on earth who has brought us more laughter and tears, who has made us proud to be Armenian? Beginning with "The Daring Young Man on the Flying Trapeze" written as a young man of 26, through "The Time of Your Life" for which he refused the Pulitzer Prize, saying he wouldn't be patronized, to "Places Where I've Done Time," William Saroyan has earned literary immortality -- the true peer of Shaw and Hemingway. As the man and his works so well remind us, William Saroyan, the seeker of simple truths, raconteur and majestic loner, is above all, a lover of humanity.

Rouben ter Arutunian

Theatrical Design - Designer. Here is one of the rare creative forces in the exciting cosmos of dance, opera, theatre and television. The inevitable rightness and drama of his scenery and costume designs have enchanted audiences in the fine arts capitals of the world. Winner of an Emmy among other coveted awards, Rouben Ter-Arutunian is as versatile as he is prolific, as attested by his remarkable list of credits in every theatrical medium. As to his artistry, Gian Carlo Menotti said it best: "There is surely something of the magician in him; he can handle space with an illusionary grace little short of miraculous...a stage designer not only with taste but ideas."

Sarkes Tarzian

Business and Industry Founder, Sarkes Tarzian, Inc. The dedication he has shown in his chosen field is exceeded by his dedication to creating a better understanding of our ideals. Innumerable homes throughout the nation have been touched through his pioneering work in broadcast electronics both present and future generations are indebted to the spirit and inventiveness of Sarkes Tarzian. He has broght the same leadership shown in his professional field to many charitable, cultural and educational endeavors for a broad spectrum of voluntary activity -- including the founding of the Chair for Armenian studies at the University of Pennsylvania. His many awards are ample evidence that in everything he has given the best of himself.

Richard Yardumian

Music Composer. Son of the Reverend Haig Yardumian, the great beacon of hope who guided hundreds of war-ravaged Armenians to America's shores Richard Yardumian is the product of a deeply religious and musical family. Few men have been able to perceive and master as many sides of music as has this internationally prized composer. With works of ever-present spirituality and supreme beauty in the forms of symphony, concerti, oratorio and chamber music, his "Come, Creator Spirit," commissioned by Fordham University, was the first setting of the Mass in the English vernacular. Equally significant, a theme from his "Armenian Suite" was the signature for the "Voice of America" broadcasts to the Soviet Union. The music of Richard Yardumian has a universal message, but speaks individually to each person. Herein lies his genius.

Barry Zorthian

Journalism - Journalist, Attorney. Barry Zorthian is one of America's most distinguished journalists. Now the Vice President for Government Affairs for Time, Inc., his meteoric career has included such executive posts as the United States' chief of press relations in Saigon. There, he became the first director of the Joint U.S. Public Affairs Office and Counselor of Embassy for Information, achieving the rank of Minister. In his four continuous years of duty in Viet Nam, he served under three U.S. Ambassadors and received the U.S.I.A.'s Distinguished Service Award. A Yale man with an LL.B. cum laude from New York University Law School, and a World War II Marine Colonel, Barry Zorthian yet shares his superb gift for leadership as a director for a host of charitable and professional organizations.

APPENDICES
Armenian Proverbs and Sayings

ARMENIAN PROVERBS AND SAYINGS

ACHIEVEMENT: If you want to achieve great things, start with
                 the small one first.

BLIND: The blind do not care whether the candles are
                 expensive or cheap.

CAT: What is play to a cat is death to a mouth.

DOGS: Dogs may quarrel among themselves, but against
                 wolfs they are united.

DRESS: A dress that is not worn wears itself out.

FLOWER: The same flower feeds a bee with honey and a
                 serpent with poison.

FOOL: When a fool throws himself into the river, even
                 forty wise men cannot pull him out.

GOD: When God gives He gives with both hands.

INTELLIGENCE: It is better to have an intelligent enemy than
                 a stupid friend.

KING: A king must be worthy of his crown.

NEIGHBOR: A close neighbor is better than a distant rela-
                 tive.

SPEECH: When you'll speak less you'll certainly hear
                 more.

SPRING: One blossom does not make spring.

THIEF: He who steals an egg today is tempted to steal
                 a horse tomorrow.

TROUBLE: Childless couples have one trouble, but couples
                 who have children have a thousand troubles.

UNKNOWN: Before you go inside an unknown place, first
                 consider how you are going to come out of it.

UNDERSTANDING: A poor man always understands better than
                 others the troubles of his peers.

WORLD: The world is like a staircase on which some go
                 up, while others go down.

BIBLIOGRAPHY

GENERAL BIBLIOGRAPHY

Brown, Francis and Joseph Roucek. <u>One America</u>: <u>the History</u>, <u>Con-</u>
<u>tributions</u> <u>and</u> <u>Present</u> <u>Problems</u> <u>of</u> <u>Our</u> <u>Racial</u> <u>and</u> <u>National</u>
<u>Minorities</u>. New York: Prentice-Hall, Inc. 1952. Short
background information on Armenian Americans and bibliography.

Federal Writers Project. <u>Armenians</u> <u>in</u> <u>Massachusetts</u>. Boston,
Massachusetts: 1937. Good coverage on the Armenian Amer-
ican community in Massachusetts, its history, achievements,
social, economic, political life and other relevant aspects. Reprinted in 1975.

Hutchinson, E.P. <u>Immigrants</u> <u>and</u> <u>Their</u> <u>Children</u>: <u>1850-1950</u>. New
York: John Wiley & Sons, Inc., 1956. Brings to light im-
portant social and economic aspects of Armenian immigration
in connection with and in comparison to other ethnic groups.
Based on the official 1950 U.S. Census data.

Mahakian, Charles. <u>History</u> <u>of</u> <u>the</u> <u>Armenians</u> <u>in</u> <u>California</u>. Los
Angeles, California: R & E Research Associates, 1974. Doc-
toral thesis based on extensive research, accompanied by
good bibliography.

Malcolm, M. Vartan. <u>The</u> <u>Armenians</u> <u>in</u> <u>America</u>. Boston-Chicago:
The Pilgrim Press, 1919. Very good coverage on Armenian
American immigration, history, adaptability in America,
religion, education, associations, political parties and
press. Considered basic book, it was reprinted in 1969.

Our Boys Committee of the Armenian General Benevolent Union of
America, Inc. <u>Armenian-American</u> <u>Veterans</u> <u>of</u> <u>World</u> <u>War</u> <u>II</u>.
New York: Armenian General Benevolent Union of America,
Inc., 1951. Well illustrated and documented 500 page
volume devoted to Armenian Americans who served with the
U.S. Armed Forces during World War II. Appended by a
short outline of Armenian history.

Tashjian, James H. <u>The</u> <u>Armenian</u> <u>American</u> <u>in</u> <u>World</u> <u>War</u> <u>II</u>. Boston,
Massachusetts: Hairenik Association, Inc., 1953. A very
extensive and well presented chronicle of the contributions
made by the Armenian Americans during World War II. Appended by tales from the war, a list of Armenian American
service women, Armenian American civil activities, participation during the Korean War.

Tashjian, James H. <u>The</u> <u>Armenians</u> <u>of</u> <u>the</u> <u>United</u> <u>States</u> <u>and</u> <u>Canada</u>.
Boston, Massachusetts: Armenian Youth Federation, 1947.
Brief but good survey on Armenian immigration to the United
States, life in America, organizations, religion, press,

and contributions to America. Accompanied by illustrations,
bibliography, and a list of prominent Armenian Americans.

SPECIAL BIBLIOGRAPHY

Ancient Civilization and Culture

Nersessian, Sirapie Der. The Armenians. New York-Washington:
Praeger Publishers, 1970. Comprehensive, clear and handy
information on the history of Armenia, Armenian social
organization, religion, literature and learning, architecture, sculpture and painting. Extensive bibliography
and relevant illustrations.

Autobiographies

Arlen, Michael J. Passage to Ararat. New York: Farrar and Strauss,
1975. The author tells his own struggle to discover the
Armenian heritage touring Armenian immigrant enclaves, talking with William Saroyan and several other personalities.

Mardikian, George. Song of America. New York: McGraw-Hill, 1956.
A very interesting book expressing the author's feelings for
America from a patriotic viewpoint.

Surmelian, Leon Z. I Ask You, Ladies and Gentlemen. New York:
Dutton, 1945. A successful autobiography portraying the
gruesome, tragic, and triumphant story of the Armenian
massacres at the hands of the Turks.

Cooking

Hogrogian, Rachel. The Armenian Cooking, New York: Atheneum,
1971. Armenian cuisine presented in all its varieties.
Accompanied by a directory of shops for buying Armenian
ingredients.

Urezian, Sonia. The Cuisine of Armenia. New York: Harper and
Row, 1974. The exciting side of Armenian cooking described
along with the influences brought from Iran, Turkey,
Lebanon, and the Caucasus.

Fiction

Hagopian, Richard. Faraway the Spring. New York: Scribner, 1952.
A very good novel devoted to the life of an Armenian American immigrant struggling to find his place in the newly
adopted country.

Housepian, Marjorie. A Houseful of Love. New York: Random
House, 1957. A very interesting, realistic portrayal

of typical Armenian American life.

Saroyan, William. My Name is Aram. New York: Harcourt, 1940.
Imaginative life of an Armenian boy in California, based
on the author's personal experiences.

Literature of the Past and Literary Criticism

Arnot, Robert and T.B. Collins, ed. Armenian Literature. New
York: The Colonial Press, 1901. General and short coverage of Armenian folklore, poetry, drama, classical traditions.

Balakian, Nona. A New Accent in American Fiction: The Armenian
American Writer. New York: Armenian General Benevolent
Union of America, 1958. Good presentation of major Ar-
menian American writers, and criticism of their work.

Manuscripts

Der Nersessian, Sirapie. Armenian Manuscripts in the Free Gallery of Art. Washington, D.C.: Smithsonian Institution,
Freer Gallery of Art (Oriental Studies No. 6), 1963.
Scientific and detailed study devoted to Armenian manuscripts going back to the 12th-17th centuries. Accompanied
by 108 plates and very extensive bibliography.

Samjian, Avedis Krikor. A Catalogue of Medieval Armenian Manuscripts in the United States. Berkeley: University of
California Press, 1976. A description of Armenian manuscripts in our country, valuable tool for researchers.

Music

Hovhannisian, Harpik Der. Armenian Music: A Cosmopolitan Art.
Tallahassee, Florida: Florida State University, 1956. A
disertatio dealing with the nature of Armenian music,
(vol. 1), and a collection of vocal and instrumental
Armenian music, both traditional and composed. (vol. 2)

Paelian, G. H. ed. Songs of Armenia. New York: The Gotchank Publication Company, 1919. Collection of Armenian folk songs,
music, and words in Armenian and English.

Poladian, Sirvart. Armenian Folk Songs. Berkeley, California:
University of California Press, 1942. Armenian music,
bibliography.

Suni, Grikor Mirzoeff. Armenian Song Bouquet. Philadelphia:
1941-1942. The author's original compositions, solos and
four part choruses, with piano accompaniment.

Organizations

Fisk, Margaret et al. ed. <u>Encyclopedia</u> <u>of</u> <u>Associations</u>. Detroit,
    Michigan: Gale Research Company, 1976. Lists Armenian Amer-
    ican organizations, and describes their specific activities.

Wynar, Lubomir ed. <u>Directory</u> <u>of</u> <u>Ethnic</u> <u>Organizations</u>. Littleton,
    Colorado: Libraries Unlimited, Inc. 1975. Very good cover-
    age on Armenian American organizations.

Periodicals

Wynar, Lubomir, ed. <u>Encyclopedic</u> <u>Directory</u> <u>of</u> <u>Ethnic</u> <u>Newspapers</u>
    <u>and</u> <u>Periodicals</u> <u>in</u> <u>the</u> <u>United</u> <u>States</u>. Littleton, Colorado:
    Libraries Unlimited, Inc. 1972. Annotates of Armenian
    American periodicals and newspapers. A revised edition
    appeared in 1976.

Poetry

Basmadjain, Garig, ed. <u>Armenian-American</u> <u>Poets</u>: <u>A</u> <u>Bilingual</u>
    <u>Anthology</u>. Southfield, Michigan: Alex Manoogian Cultural
    Fund of the Armenian General Benevolent Union, 1976.
    First bilingual anthology devoted to Armenian-American poets
    ever to be published in the U.S.A. It embraces poems writ-
    ten by twenty-one American and Canadian poets, and it is
    appended by biographical notes.

Radio Stations

American Council for Nationalities Service. <u>Foreign</u> <u>Language</u>
    <u>Radio</u> <u>Stations</u> <u>in</u> <u>the</u> <u>U.S.A.</u> New York: 1970. Lists all
    radio stations broadcasting Armenian language programs.

Religion

Jaquet, Constant H. <u>Yearbook</u> <u>of</u> <u>American</u> <u>and</u> <u>Canadian</u> <u>Churches</u>:
    <u>1976</u>. Nashville, Tennessee: Abingdon Press, 1976. Fur-
    nishes up to date statistical data on denominations to
    which Armenian Americans belong, as well as the way they
    are organized.

Mead, Frank S., ed. <u>Handbook</u> <u>of</u> <u>Denominations</u> <u>in</u> <u>the</u> <u>United</u>
    States. Nashville, Tennessee: Abingdon Press, 1970. De-
    scribes the organizational structure of the Armenian
    Church.

PERIODICAL LITERATURE

Ferretti, Fred "Armenians Give Historic Tapestries to New York"
    <u>The</u> <u>New</u> <u>York</u> <u>Times</u>, September 11, 1976.

Fosburgh, Lacey "Armenians Here Rediscovering Rich Heritage" The
    New York Times, July 16, 1969.

Ricklets, Roger "Small Ethnic Groups Enjoy Revived Interest in
    Cultural Heritage" The Wall Street Journal, July 11, 1973.

Saroyan, William "Shout Armenia Wherever You Go" Saturday Evening
    Post, November 21, 1964.

Saroyan, William "Our Greatest Man" Saturday Evening Post, March
    12, 1966.

DISCOGRAPHY

Armenian Choral Music, Folkways, FW 8704, with the Armenian Na-
    tional Choral Society of Boston, Massachusetts, conducted
    by Siranoush Der-Manuelian.

Armenian Liturgical Music, Cosmopolitan Chorale, Florence Mardiros-
    ian conductor; Westminster XTV 18970/71.

Armenian Mass, Westminster, WN 18726, with the Lord's Prayer, the
    hymn of vesting, the hagiology, and others.

Armenian Songs, Westminster & WN 18824, folk songs and choruses
    performed by the Cosmopolitan Chorale conducted by Florence
    Mardirosian.

Symphony Etchmiadzin and Armenian Rhapsody No. 3, Poseidon Society
    1004, performed by the Royal Philarmonic Orchestra of Great
    Britain, and conducted by composer Alan Hovhanes.

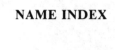

NAME INDEX

NAME INDEX